Listen, My Son

To my Father

Listen, My Son
St Benedict for Fathers

DWIGHT LONGENECKER

MOREHOUSE PUBLISHING
Harrisburg, Pennsylvania

First Published 2000
Gracewing
2 Southern Avenue
Leominster, Herefordshire HR6 0QF
England

Morehouse Publishing
P.O. Box 1321
Harrisburg, PA 17105

Morehouse Publishing is a division of The Morehouse Group.

Translation of *The Rule of St Benedict*, the estate of Abbot Parry, OSB.

Cover design by Tom Castanzo

Printed in the United States of America
05 06 07 08   10 9 8 7 6 5 4 3 2

Library of Congress Cataloging-in-Publication Data

Longenecker, Dwight
Listen My Son: St Benedict for Fathers/ Dwight Longenecker.
    p. cm
Includes bibliographical references.
ISBN 0-8192-1856-1(pbk.: alk. paper)
    1. Benedict, Saint, Abbot of Monte Cassino. Regula. 2. Fatherhood—Religious aspects—Catholic Church. I. Title.

BX3004.Z5 L66 2000
255'.106-dc21

99-086446

CONTENTS

FOREWORD

In his writings, Pope John Paul II contrasts two things – the civilization of love and the culture of death. He highlights the basic struggle between good and evil, right and wrong. The Pope is saying, 'Look at the contrast between destruction, violence, and death – all under the name of choice, but all about selfishness, all about rights, all about me putting myself first – look at the contrast between that and the civilization of love, which is based on the idea of community and love.'

The most basic community is the family. Jacques Maritain, a great Catholic philosopher, taught that each person is made in the image of God. Each human being is unique and therefore to be intimately respected. He resisted the philosophy of individualism. For Maritain the human personality is at the heart of the equation. People are formed into communities and the most basic is the family. The family then becomes a neighbourhood, the workplace, school, institution, whatever it may be, and within those communities you may make things work by giving something of yourself. That to me is the civilization of love; it is giving something of yourself and not always expecting to have everything for your benefit.

It is no wonder that Pope Paul VI named St Benedict the patron of Europe. He saw that in Benedict's Rule were the foundations of a civilization of love. In the Rule, Benedict calls his brother monks not only to obedience to the rightful authority, but also to mutual obedience, based on their love for one another. This is the love which Christ has for us since he was sent 'not to be served, but to serve, and to give his life as a ransom for many'. This same mutual self-giving love is at the heart of the Christian marriage, and the Christian home. When it begins to live there, it spreads outward to the whole of society.

Historically we can see how this happened through the Rule of St Benedict. The Rule was written in the dark days of the sixth century, when the Roman Empire – rotten with decadence from within – was finally crumbling into chaos. Benedict's 'little Rule' became the foundation document for the monasteries which became the oases of love, learning and light for the next thousand years. The monasteries kept alive the ideas and learning of earlier civilizations but they also generated a new ideal: civilization based not on military might, but on worship, service and love. Theirs was an attempt to build Christ's Kingdom, which flourished for a thousand years and still thrives quietly today.

The wisdom of Benedict is timeless. His words are completely incarnational, blending practical wisdom with profound spiritual insight. Neither are Benedict's words simply for monks and nuns. More and more laypeople around the world are finding guidance, inspiration and encouragement by following the way of Benedict.

In his book, Dwight Longenecker has provided a daily commentary on the Rule of St Benedict for fathers. In the UK alone, where 800,000 children have no contact with their fathers, we need a parable to facilitate the return of the lost fathers. Perhaps this is it. But although his focus is on fathers, the commentary applies Benedict's practical wisdom to every family situation; indeed, Benedict's insights apply not only within the home or monastery, but wherever people struggle to live, work and pray together. Benedict wrote before the great divisions of the Reformation. His words are simple, Scriptural and universal. I recommend this book to Christian parents of all traditions as they seek to build strong Christian families which will, in turn, be the building blocks of a civilization of love.

Lord David Alton

PREFACE

Whenever I write or speak about religion a certain story of Jesus' echoes in my mind. It is the one where he points to the Pharisees who 'love to wear long robes and sit in the best seats in the temple and make long prayers'. This is never more true than when writing about spirituality, and the excruciating crunch of Christ's words has pressed home even more as I have written about the vocation of being a Christian husband and father.

I am only too aware that what I have said about the Christian family is idealistic, and that the reality of our own home is far from the ideal. Gregory the Great said about Benedict, 'He could not have written what he did not live'. I doubt if someone reviewing my life could be quite so optimistic. My wife is the first to point out that I don't live up to my own good words, but I think she admits that even if I don't succeed, at least I'm making the effort. I hope in our better moments we can have a laugh together and say with the old monk who was asked what they do in the monastery, 'We fall and get up, fall and get up, fall and get up again'.

So this book is not about my attainments, but my aims. It is written from my own experience of growing up in a Christian family. It is also written from the experience of trying to follow the way of Benedict for about fifteen years, first as an Anglican minister and now as a Catholic layman. It also comes out of my own experience in the 'thick of things' with four young children: Benedict, Madeleine, Theodore and Elias. It could not have been written without them and it certainly could not have been considered without my wife, whose example in self-giving teaches me every day. Without them I would be a solitary hermit. With them I am a faltering abbot.

If I have had the courage to attempt fatherhood and to attempt to write on it, then I have my own father to thank. Indeed, if I have any Christian faith at all I have him to thank. He and my mother brought up five children in an evangelical tradition to 'know and love the Lord'. As a result each one of us has kept the faith and managed to build our own Christian marriages and families the best we know how. In this day and age my parents' success is a noteworthy accomplishment. My father knew nothing about St Benedict, but his example of fatherhood was close to the Benedictine ideal I set out here. He was strict but understanding. When he said, 'This hurts me more than it hurts you ...', we believed it. He taught us to respect physical things and one another. He always stressed the need for good stewardship, balance and gentleness of mind. Most of all he was unfailing in his spiritual life. He led the family in prayer and we saw him pray. We knew he gave sacrificially. We saw him get involved in the local church, in the international church and in Christian mission. Because his faith was real and active we have faith today, for children do what their parents do, not necessarily what their parents say.

Finally, if I presume to comment on the sacred Rule of St Benedict I must thank June, a Benedictine oblate, who first encouraged me to visit a monastery over twenty years ago. Among many monastic friends, the late Abbot of Quarr, Dom Leo Avery, was a humble father and spiritual guide. Dom Joseph McNerney gave friendship and proved an intelligent and understanding pastor on our journey into the Catholic Church. The community at Mont St Michel have always given me a warm Gallic welcome, and the monks at Downside Abbey, especially Dom Daniel

Rees, have encouraged and helped me with this text. Finally, Dom Laurence Kelly shows me a life full of grace, wisdom and joy. He is the old porter who opens the door for me with a word of thanks and blessing.

Dwight Longenecker
Chippenham
The Feast of St Joseph
19 March 1999

INTRODUCTION

The Challenge of Fatherhood
When St Benedict says, 'Listen my son to the advice of a loving father' he calls us into an intimate child–parent relationship. The need to be nurtured and guided through life doesn't cease when we reach the magic age of eighteen. In every stage of life we need the wisdom, concern and love of a father figure. If we are fathers ourselves, the need for a mentor is even greater. We cannot be good fathers if we do not have a good father in our own life.

Jesus taught us to call God 'father' and this teaching flowed from his own intimate relationship with God the father. Jesus called God 'Abba' or 'papa'. With such an intimate term he reveals the tenderness and strength which should exist between fathers and children, and between us and our heavenly father. In recent years the concept of fatherhood has lost its attraction, and some people view fathers as the source of every ill in society. Of course many have suffered at the hands of poor fathers. Many have also suffered from inadequate mothering. But the failure of some fathers does not negate the need for positive, potent and compassionate fatherhood. Indeed bad fathering makes the need for good fathers even more acute. The foundation of successful fathering is a living relationship with God the Father. It is only from a dynamic spiritual relationship with him that human fathers can hope to do their very best for their children.

This primary relationship with God the Father can be nurtured and developed through the spiritual fathers we find within the family of the church. In a spiritual director or wise confessor God gives us a spiritual father to help us on our journey. Like St Jospeh, our spiritual director adopts us as his own. He protects and provides for us until we reach maturity. St Benedict has been a spiritual father for countless men and women for well over fifteen hundred years. Through his little rule generations of monks, nuns and lay people have heard the voice of a wise and loving father who wishes to guide them to perfection.

A guide for fathers is vital today since fatherhood has been so neglected. Christian fathers especially need resources to foster their paternal role. Many men in our society are confused and bewildered by a whole array of contradictory expectations. Short-term contracts, performance-related pay and high pressure competition pushes fatherhood into second place. On the one hand, the 'new man' is expected to be the perfect father and husband, while the voices of those who may have been injured by bad fathering often portray all fathers as domineering villains.

Quick divorce and re-marriage, along with the financial attraction of co-habitation, and a mentality which separates sexuality from procreation encourage many men to avoid marriage and fatherhood altogether, or to walk out on the family once the stresses of real family life begin to develop. The younger generation of men can hardly be blamed. Many young men are themselves the product of broken homes, where in most cases it was the father who was the absent parent. Without a father it is impossible for them to be fathers.

However, within this grim scenario there is cause for great hope. Fatherhood may be neglected and despised, but there are signs of a swing back. In all sorts of low-key ways men are returning to the priority of parenting. In larger enterprises which cross cultural and religious boundaries men are being encouraged to take their domestic responsibilities seriously; to return to their families and to take up the challenge of compassionate leadership within the home. Men who have been excluded from their homes and children by harsh divorce laws are fighting back for the rights of fathers. Through marriage guidance, counselling and self-help programmes thousands of men are learning new ways of relating to their wives and families, and finding renewal in the heart of their homes. In addition, an increasing number of firms are recognizing the need for paternity leave, shorter hours and proper responses to family requirements; recognizing that a man who is fulfilled at home is a better and more productive worker. Many men who work for impersonal multinational firms are discovering that it is within family life that they have true identity, and there they discover a sense of belonging and a true vocation.

This return to fatherhood should not be seen as an attempt to turn the clock back. If an old patriarchy has died it is so that a better view of fatherhood can be resurrected. The new fatherhood is not a return to an antiquated patriarchy in which the man is king and the woman a mere chattel. Instead the new father is caring, involved and fully integrated into the life of the family. The new father relates with his wife on equal terms. There is a new interdependence and complementary self-giving which recognizes the advances in women's self-understanding as well as the demands of modern society. If the mother has had a more formative role on children in recent years, then the new father is now sharing that function in full partnership with her. If she shares the bread-winning, then he shares in the child-care. The new father is there not as the king, but as the servant–king. In fact, while this approach to fatherhood seems new, it is there in the Scriptural pattern for marriage, and St Benedict points to it in his chapter on mutual obedience. The new fatherhood does not expect obedience or respect by right, but earns respect and obedience by self-sacrifice and compassionate leadership.

This kind of fatherhood is hard work, but it pays rich dividends. Not only is the man rewarded with loyal and loving children as he grows older, but he also enjoys a deepening and more profound relationship with his wife. In addition, his children go out into the world brimming with confidence and strength from his contribution.

Finally, it is easy to see the decay and confusion in modern life and to run for cover. The instinctive response of Christian parents may be to construct a family fortress against the wicked world. But while the home is a place of refuge, it is also a place of preparation and interaction with the wider world. Parents will best protect their children from the destructive forces in the world not by running away from them, but by equipping their children to engage with the world in a creative and dynamic way. In fact, there may be no more effective way to make the world a better place than for men and women to take their responsibility as parents seriously, and so contribute members of society who are responsible, compassionate and confident.

Christian parents help to redeem and transform the world by building a good home, for good homes are the building blocks of a solid, prosperous and peaceful society. When this calling to parenthood is linked with a strong Christian vision, the home, as Tertullian said, becomes the 'seminary of the human race', and the Christian father and mother find in their parental roles a path which leads to heaven.

The Christian family can be the place for the soul's training because it is, by its nature, a Christian community. A person may choose a convent or a monastery to join, but they cannot choose every monk they have to live with; neither can they choose every successive abbot or abbess to whom they must vow obedience. Likewise, we may choose our wives or husbands, but we can't choose all our in-laws and we certainly can't choose our children. They are given to us and we must learn to live with them in community. Since Jesus first called twelve men to live in intimate community with him, the Church has been a family, a community, a Kingdom of God. So it is with the natural family: we find within our own home all the necessary ingredients for progress in the Christian life.

St John has written, 'Those who live in love live in God and God lives in them.' So within the love of the Christian family the father can come to understand and dwell in all wisdom. Through his love with his wife, the two share in a union which is as intimate as the one Christ shares with his Church. Through their relationship with the children a three-way bond is nurtured which takes each family member into a love which reflects the Holy Trinity itself, for there Father, Son and Holy Spirit exist in the perfect unity of the Divine Family. The ordinary Christian home is part of the God-given sacrament of marriage, and as in all sacraments it is a physical means of meeting the invisible God face to face.

This is a high ideal. It sounds mystical and sublime. But the reality often seems far from celestial. Being a parent is a gritty, realistic and demanding vocation. Our lives are rooted in the physical and emotional needs of small children. We need to be equipped for Christian fatherhood. There are many resources for spiritual growth, but not many which combine the practical demands of fatherhood with the aspirations of the spiritual journey. Some books are full of practical advice on parenting while others take us on a wonderful, but too other-worldly, journey of spirituality. Not many books combine practical advice with spiritual insight. *The Rule of St Benedict*, more than any other, combines the two into a fully incarnational guide to life.

The Life and Rule of St Benedict

The sixth-century Rule of St Benedict is a code written for the foundation and maintenance of a Christian monastery. It has been in use for the last fifteen hundred years as the basis for every Benedictine monastery and convent and for many other religious orders which are loosely Benedictine. Some scholars even credit Benedict and his Rule as the foundation of Western civilization, for there the basic guidelines of all community can be traced, and it was the monastic communities, following Benedict's inspiration, which kept human learning and civilization alive during the Dark Ages.

Benedict's Rule may have been written with sixth-century needs in mind, but it has stood the test of time because of Benedict's profound understanding of human psychology. Benedict understands that we need something to aspire towards, but we also need a realistic view of ourselves. We need to reach for the stars, but keep our feet on the ground. Like all works of genius, Benedict's Rule inspires and humbles us at the same time. He takes us to lofty heights, and yet his Rule is full of practical wisdom and principles of human relationship which can be applied to almost any situation where people live and work together. A serious reading of Benedict will enlighten and inspire not only our family life, but our relationships at work, in the parish, and in our wider community.

Although it was written for monks, Benedict's Rule is not a piece of mystical writing as such. It doesn't give extravagant and obscure teaching on prayer and mysticism. The Rule is a practical document for everyday living. It is modest in its aim: indeed, Benedict himself calls it a 'little Rule for beginners'. The Rule is also modest in its composition. Benedict never claims complete originality. Christian monasticism began in Egypt in the middle of the fourth century, and Benedict has drawn from the literature of those first Egyptian monks – the Desert Fathers. He also relies on the Eastern *Conferences of Cassian* and on the contemporary *Rule of the Master*. But Benedict makes his own mark. Unlike the earlier writers, Benedict promotes a new balance. He tempers monastic austerities with a gentle tolerance of human weakness. He eschews extremism and builds a Rule which strives for heaven while understanding how bound we are to earth. For Benedict heaven and earth are not in conflict; as a master of incarnational spirituality he helps us see 'heaven in ordinary'. So every material possession is to be treated as a sacred vessel of the altar, and Christ is to be seen in the abbot, every brother, and every guest of the monastery.

Benedict the Man
Benedict's Rule speaks to our time because he also wrote in a century of social upheaval and uncertainty. In AD 410 – seventy years before he was born – Rome fell to the barbarian invasions, and by the middle of the sixth century Rome had been sacked for a second time and the Huns were ravaging northern Italy. The civil authority was in tatters; wars, violence and anarchy were raging and the Church too was torn in pieces by theological controversy over the nature of grace. In the midst of this turbulent time Benedict managed to construct a way of life which rode the storm like an ark in the raging flood.

Benedict was born around 480 into a noble family of Nursia. He was sent to Rome to study, but abandoned the city because of the decadence he saw there. He went to live the hermit's life in the hills near Subiaco where he was looked after by another solitary monk. Eventually he was invited to become the abbot of a nearby monastery, but after almost being poisoned by the rebellious monks he left. He finally settled with some brothers at Monte Cassino, where the reconstructed mother house of the Benedictine order still stands today. Some distance away his sister Scholastica had established a convent of nuns, and Benedict met with her once a year. Before his death Benedict's friend and confidant, Servandus, tells us how he was summoned to Benedict's cell one night. Benedict had got up in the night to pray and he saw a bright light come down from heaven. Encapsulated in that light was the entire created order 'as if gathered into a single ray of light'. This ultimate vision of the unity of all things is the gift which is given through the life of contemplation. Benedict's Rule is a way to run on the path towards that vision of unified love. So he calls us in his Prologue to 'run on the path of God's commandments with an inexpressible delight of love'.

The life of St Benedict was written by Pope St Gregory the Great. In his *Dialogues* he records the death of St Benedict. He died on 21 March 547 in the oratory or chapel of the monastery. After receiving communion he stood with his hands raised in prayer, and died supported by his brothers. So in death he was surrounded by the community, making him a latter-day Moses whose arms were held up by Joshua and Aaron so the battle could be won. After his death, the monastery was destroyed by the invading Lombards and the traditions tell us that some monks took Benedict's remains, and those of his sister, to the Abbey of St Benoit-sur-Loire, where his relics remain today.

The Way of Benedict
In his opening Prologue Benedict calls us to make an act of the will – to take a decision to follow the path of God's commandments. After a section on different types of monks he turns to the traits of a good abbot. He goes on with a fairly traditional outline of the steps of obedience and humility, then goes on to deal with the mundane matters of running the monastery. He tells the monks how to conduct the services in chapel, how to be disciplined, how to treat the physical goods of the monastery and how to live together in peace. But woven through the whole Rule is an awareness that the rules are simply training exercises. They are designed to channel the monk's life into an inner freedom and holiness. Throughout the Rule the three Benedictine vows of Stability, Obedience and Conversion of Life provide a driving force.

Benedict sees spiritual maturity as something which is attained obliquely. Enlightenment cannot be attained on its own like the reward for some sort of esoteric quest. Like happiness, enlightenment is the product of a certain type of life. So enlightenment or spiritual wholeness is only accomplished through a lifetime of wholeness. The monk's task is to develop the atmosphere and attitude of spiritual wholeness. The monastery becomes a 'workshop' where spiritual accomplishment happens, and every rule is simply a contribution to the necessary atmosphere of wholeness. This wholeness consists of finding our proper place in the world and giving glory to God by living fully within his order, or finding, as Dante said, 'Our peace in His will'. One of the ways to find this place of simplicity and wholeness is by pursuing stability of life.

On the physical level stability simply means the monk may not go travelling around. He is enclosed and bound to his particular community for life. But inner stability means we also give up the constant search for new religious experience and spiritual fulfilment on our own terms. Stability can best be described as that state of mind which is content in the present moment. Stability accepts what is given and finds God not 'out there' but 'in here'. Many of the rules Benedict established are to help the monk stay put happily. Benedict realizes that if a person cannot find God where he is then he will not find him anywhere, and the vow of stability forces the monk to face the reality that escape is not one of the options.

The emphasis on stability is vital in our personal lives and in our Christian homes. In a fast-changing world where mobility is taken for granted it is all too easy to move house, move church or move job simply because we are bored or restless or think things will be better somewhere else. The Christian husband and father is forced into stability by his marriage vows and by the need to provide for his family. We can either rebel against these enforced 'enclosures' or we can see them as the crucible of our own spiritual refinement. The constraints of family life can either be the chains that bind us or the force of stability which gives us true freedom. Stability reminds us that we may run away from others, but we cannot run away from ourselves.

Obedience is the second of the monk's vows. If the

monk stays at home in his desire for stability, then he also does so within a local society based on obedience to a rightfully recognized authority. The monk commits himself to a relationship of obedience to his abbot. This is never obedience for its own sake. Instead, Benedict expects the monk to take a vow of obedience, because through constant obedience his self-will is broken and humility may begin to flower. Benedicts spends much time expounding the virtue of obedience because obedience counters the root sin of wilful pride and cuts to the base of that egotism which fosters all other sin. Once again, the humility which comes from obedience is not holiness itself, but it is the condition for holiness. The vow of stability and the vow of obedience both nurture humility, and with humility the ground is prepared for spiritual wholeness to grow.

If we take our marriage vows seriously then we too have the basis for a life of obedience. In our case obedience means being in a constant attitude of self-sacrificial service towards our wives and children. St Paul commands us: 'Husbands, love your wives, as Christ loves the Church and gave himself for her.' The demands of family life demand a regular sacrifice of our will and our desire for the good of others. Benedict never pretends that obedience is easy. Of the three vows this is perhaps the most difficult one to attain on our own. But Benedict always reminds us to 'put our trust completely in the Lord'. Everything we do must be fuelled by his grace – but especially the desire to learn true obedience.

Finally, the Benedictine monk makes a vow of conversion of life. This does not mean he seeks some sort of 'conversion experience'. Instead the monk lives with the aim that his whole life, body, soul and spirit, will be converted into the likeness of Christ. Thomas Merton relates a story from the Desert Fathers which points to this total transformation: Abbot Lot came to Abbot Joseph and said he was doing the best he could to observe his holy rule of life, and what more should he do? 'The elder rose up in reply and stretched out his hands to heaven and his fingers became like ten lamps of fire. He said, "Why not be totally changed into fire?"' Conversion of life means the Christian is brought to the point where he naturally says with Benedict that he 'prefers nothing to the love of Christ'. Every detail in the monk's life is subjugated to this one aim. However, this does not mean the monk is straining to convert himself. Instead, by following the Rule he simply aims to prepare the ground for this conversion, and to prepare himself to co-operate with that conversion which can only be accomplished by the grace of God.

One of the ways to prepare for and co-operate with this conversion is to develop a constant awareness of God's presence. Throughout the Rule Benedict reminds the monks to 'be awake', to 'be alert' and watchful for the Lord's presence. This watchful awareness of God is a humble state of dependence on the heavenly Father. To nurture this awareness of God is also to nurture humility because an awareness of God reveals our own frail condition. Awareness also leads to an attentiveness to our daily lives as 'sacraments of the present moment'. Awareness of God's presence becomes an awareness of his loving Spirit in all things and all people. Then as G.M. Hopkins has written, the whole 'world is charged with the glory of God'.

This is possible within our daily lives as it is within the ordinary existence in the monastery. As laymen we are called by virtue of our baptism to 'prefer nothing to the love of Christ'. We may not achieve our own conversion of life, but we can co-operate with God's grace and prepare the ground for that work which he is pleased to do within us. The demands of our marriage and family life are more than enough to lead us to that total conversion which God provides through Jesus Christ.

How to Use This Book
The Rule of St Benedict has been followed by monks and nuns for the last fifteen hundred years. Increasingly the

Rule is also being used by laypeople. As a guide for Christian fathers it is indispensable. The Rule is intended for abbots in the monastery, and the word 'abbot' is based on the Aramaic *abba* which Christ himself uses for God the Father. As such the Rule instructs abbots how to run the monastery, and the wisdom of the Rule is easily applied to the *abba* – or father within the Christian home. Benedict's tender compassion for his charges reflects the love we feel for our children. His shrewd understanding of human nature resonates with our own experience, both as children and fathers. So Benedict offers some wise advice about discipline, but he is also forever warm-hearted and compassionate. Benedict helps weak fathers to be stronger and challenges strict fathers to be more gentle. Benedict never compromises the high ideals, but he also never forces anyone to assume a burden which may be too heavy.

This commentary is specially designed for busy Christian fathers. But while the focus is on the father's role, the emphasis is on the whole family. As Benedict's Rule is a guide both for abbots and for the whole community, so this is a book to be shared: indeed nothing would be better than for husbands and wives to read it together. While it seeks to support fathers, and doesn't mention the mother's role very much, this is not to pretend that her role is negligible – only that this book discusses the work of both parents by focusing on the father. It assumes an underlying unity between husband and wife and that both father and mother are working together as 'one body' for the welfare and proper training of the children. In that respect most of what is written here applies to both parents.

Benedict's Rule* is broken down into daily readings which spread the whole Rule over four months. This is the breakdown which is used in most monasteries and convents, so as the reader goes through the Rule three times in one year he reads in solidarity with the monks

The Rule of St Benedict, translated by Abbot Parry OSB (Gracewing, Leominster, 1997).

and nuns. Along with each daily reading is a short meditation which applies the Rule to Christian family life. Part of the Benedictine monk's life consists of *lectio divina*, or inspirational reading. The Christian father, if he is to take his vocation seriously, needs to have some regular spiritual input as well. A short portion of the Benedictine Rule combined with a practical meditation helps to draw out the spiritual significance of the Rule and apply Benedict's wisdom to the needs of modern family life.

Benedict's Rule is also imbued with Scripture, especially the Psalms. Benedict doesn't use Scripture to provide proof texts for his argument. Instead Benedict worships with Scripture, meditates on Scripture and prays with Scripture. The words of the Scriptures are written on Benedict's heart, and so within the Rule he quotes Scripture in bits and pieces, making passing reference to passages which his hearers would know well. We are not as familiar with Scripture as they were, so Scripture references are provided within the text of the commentary for further reference and meditation. The reader who wishes to push further into Benedict's wisdom will do well to read this commentary with the Scriptures close at hand. It may do to simply pick out one Scripture reference for the day and read it along with its whole context. This will weave Scripture reading into Benedict's Rule in a way which will not only improve the reader's Bible knowledge, but will also help him apply the living Scriptures to his daily life in a dynamic way.

Finally, this book is not meant to be an easy or a quick read. The tradition of *lectio divina* is that of prayerful, slow and meditative reading. So each day's text from the Rule, the meditation and the Scripture references are meant to key a somewhat longer time of meditation and contemplation. In a busy life it may not be possible to take more than a few lines. There is nothing wrong with that as long as those few thoughts are taken with the reader through the day. Since a slow and meditative reading is recommended it should also follow that one read through is not enough.

It should be read through at least three times in one full
year. The monks read the Rule over and over again. It
wouldn't hurt us to do the same.

This book may also be the start for more laymen and
women to follow the Benedictine way in their own homes.
To follow the way most fully it is a good idea to establish
contact with a monastery or convent close to home. Most
religious houses are pleased to welcome men and women
for retreats and will guide newcomers to this tradition. In
addition there is the opportunity to become an oblate of a
Benedictine convent or monastery. An oblate is similar to
a third order Franciscan: they maintain a close link with
the religious house, supporting the monks or nuns in their
vocation and drawing strength from the friendship and
support which the monastery has to offer. Thus together
the religious celibate and the married layman complement
one another's calling as they run together on the 'path of
God's commandments with an inexpressible delight of
love'.

THE PROLOGUE (A)

Listen my son to the instructions of your Master, turn the ear of your heart to the advice of a loving father; accept it willingly and carry it out vigorously; so that through the toil of obedience you may return to him from whom you have separated by the sloth of disobedience.

To you, then, whoever you may be, are my words addressed, who, by the renunciation of your own will, are taking up the strong and glorious weapons of obedience in order to do battle in the service of the Lord Christ, the true King.

First of all, whenever you begin any good work, you must ask of God with the most urgent prayer that it may be brought to completion by him, so that he, who has now deigned to reckon us in the number of his sons, may not later on be made sad by our wicked actions. For we must at all times use the good gifts he has placed in us, so that he will not later on disinherit us as an angry father disinherits his sons; nor like a feared lord, who has been roused to anger by our sins, hand over to eternal punishment us wicked slaves for refusing to follow him to glory.

⌘

From the first words of the Rule, Benedict speaks to us as a loving father and calls us into a relationship with our heavenly Father. The theme of fatherhood runs through Benedict's whole Rule, for the abbot is the father of the monastic community. As such he stands in the place of Christ, and in Benedict's day theologians spoke much of Christ as the 'father' of the new humanity. Like the abbot, the cellarer too is called to be 'a father to the whole community'. So Benedict sees the monastic community as a loving Christian family, and his Rule can be read as an invaluable guide for the Christian family even today.

As our loving father in God Benedict calls us first of all to engage our will, so we may set off on the path of holiness. The main obstacle to our spiritual progress is inertia, or sloth. Sloth is not just slovenly laziness. Instead it is a state of mind which is unable to take spiritual action. It is a spiritual torpor, disinterestedness and complacency. Benedict makes clear that this spiritual condition is a deadly downward spiral. Such inertia is caused by disobedience and causes further disobedience.

If disobedience is the cause of spiritual torpor, then obedience is the remedy (cf. Bar. 4.28). So Benedict rouses us with a new call to take up 'the strong and glorious weapons of obedience in order to do battle in the service of the Lord Christ'. It is unfashionable in an age of relativistic individualism to call for obedience, but the gospel has always called individuals to submit their will to God's (Matt. 6.10). Benedict calls us to engage our will, but he also encourages us because it is God who is at work in us bringing his will to completion in us (Phil. 2.12–13).

This call to obedience is one of the three foundation stones of the Benedictine life. The Rule opens by calling us to attention with the word 'listen' and it is no coincidence that the root of the word 'obey' is 'to hear or listen'. So the kind of obedience called for is not the childish, mindless obedience of the military drone, but an obedience which first attentively seeks to understand. So we are to 'turn the ear of [our] heart to the advice of a loving father'.

As Christian fathers we rightly expect obedience from our children (Eph. 6.1). The fool expects mindless obedience by virtue of force. But the loving father – like Benedict himself – nurtures an open-hearted, attentive and intelligent obedience in which the will is fully engaged and attracted by love.

THE PROLOGUE (B)

Let us then at last arouse ourselves, even as Scripture incites us in the words, 'Now is the hour for us to rise from sleep.' Let us, then, open our eyes to the divine light, and hear with our ears the divine voice as it cries out to us daily. 'Today if you hear his voice, do not harden your hearts,' and again, 'He who has ears to hear, let him hear what the Spirit says to the Churches.' And what does the Spirit say? 'Come, my sons, listen to me; I shall teach you the fear of the Lord.' 'Run while you have the light of life lest the darkness of death overwhelm you.'

Benedict calls us from spiritual inertia to spiritual initiative; from complacency to action. But there is more here than the summons to a life of faithful good works. Benedict's call to holiness is an alarm – a wake-up call. Like St Paul, Benedict is calling us to rise out of sleep (Rom. 13.11).

All the spiritual traditions teach that the unenlightened state is like being asleep. It has never been more true than in contemporary Western society. Sometimes it seems that the whole modern world is conspiring to weave a magical spell over us. Television, advertising, and all the tools of popular culture continually bombard us with seductive and hypnotic false images. If we are not careful, this false culture can dull our senses and lull us into a kind of trance, and we begin to exist in a nether world of attractive lies and half-truths.

Benedict calls us to awake out of this dozy world and face reality. Beginning the spiritual journey means we must wake up and see ourselves and our world for the first time. We must listen intently to the divine voice which cries out daily (Ps. 95.8). This profound openness to God's voice and God's way of seeing requires a radical transformation in our whole viewpoint. It is like seeing in colour when once we saw in black and white.

To live in this wakeful state is the work of a lifetime, and for the first time Benedict says we must 'run' in this path. Run, while you have the light, he says, lest the darkness of death overtake you (John 12.35). Running is an apt metaphor for the spiritual life because running is a discipline which is both exhausting and exhilarating. To run in Benedict's way is to practise the difficult art of contemplation – the art of being spiritually awake and alert.

This sounds the stuff of mystical retreats in caves, but the alert state of mind is most simply cultivated through daily prayer and thankfulness (Col. 4.2). A moment of genuine gratitude to God is a moment of contemplation because in that moment, as in contemplation, we look beyond ourselves in love. As Julian of Norwich writes, 'Thanksgiving is the deep inward certainty which moves us with reverent and loving fear to turn with all our strength to the work which God stirs us, giving thanks and praise from the depth of our hearts.'

So as we nurture a thankful spirit in ourselves and in our homes, we lay the foundations for the contemplative life. Therefore, the child's first prayer ought to be the simple prayer of thanks. And as we grow to thank God for the small things, it is not long before our awareness grows and we are able to contemplate his mighty hand in all his works.

THE PROLOGUE (C)

*And as the Lord seeks his workman in the mass of people, he
again cries out to him in the words, 'Who is the man who desires
life and is eager to see Good Days?' If you hear this and reply, 'I
do', God says to you, 'If you want to have true and everlasting
life, keep your tongue from speaking evil, and your lips from
uttering deceit. Turn aside from evil and do good; seek peace and
follow after it.' 'When you do this my eyes will be upon you, and
my ears will be open to your prayers, and before you call upon
me I shall say to you: "Here I am".' What can be sweeter to us
than this voice of the Lord as he invites us, dearest brothers? See
how, in his loving mercy, the Lord points out to us the Way of
Life.*

⁊

Developing a thankful spirit in the home is one of the
simplest and most effective ways of promoting an awareness of God's presence and constant love. One hears a lot
about the power of positive thinking, but positive thinking
on its own is little more than a kind of self-hypnosis.
Thankfulness, on the other hand, is God-directed positive
thinking.

This kind of spiritually-positive attitude is something
Benedict stresses in today's passage from the Rule. The
disciple is one who 'desires life and is eager to see good
days'. This kind of disciple keeps his tongue from speaking evil and his lips from uttering deceit. He turns aside
from evil and does good; he seeks peace and follows after
it (Ps. 34.12–15). Those persons who are running the path

with Benedict have a positive outlook because they look for the good not the evil. They seek peace, not conflict. This is supplemented by their thankful attitude because thankfulness helps them see the good side of every person and circumstance.

This isn't to say that the monastery or the Christian home should be a saccharine centre of falsely-grinning Christians. Nothing rings more untrue than artificial religious enthusiasm, and there is no such thing as a community without conflict. However, some people do imagine that the suppression of all anger and bad-tempered outbursts make a home Christian. In fact, this only leads to a false peace and a deeper kind of evil. It does so because the suppression of all conflict and human unpleasantness is an insidious form of untruthfulness.

Benedict doesn't allow such an outwardly pleasant lie. While he stresses that we should keep our lips from speaking evil he also says they should not utter deceit. So conflict must be handled honestly. Anger must be acknowledged and dealt with. The parents who seek peace will also seek justice, knowing that much anger flows from a perception that justice has not been done. The family who seeks this combination of peace and justice, honesty and speaking no evil is bound to flourish. Spiritually speaking, God is right next to them, and promises to hear even before they ask (Isa. 58.6–11).

Benedict is optimistic and moved by the possibilities this promises. He has lifted much of the Prologue from earlier monastic writings, but here his own tender personality shines through in the words *fratres carissimi* – 'dearest brothers'. So he calls us with simple and winning enthusiasm as his own dear brothers to listen to the voice of the Lord and to run with him in the path of Christ's abundant life (Ps. 25.10; John 10.10).

THE PROLOGUE (D)

Let us therefore make for ourselves a girdle out of faith and perseverance in good works, and under the guidance of the Gospel let us pursue our way in his paths, so that we may deserve to see him who has called us to his Kingdom. For if we wish to make our home in the dwelling-place of his Kingdom, there will be no getting there unless we run towards it by good deeds. But let us question the Lord with the prophet, saying to him, 'Lord, who shall make his home in your dwelling-place; who shall rest on your holy mountain?' And then let us listen to the Lord's answer to our question, as he shows us the way to this dwelling-place, saying, 'He who walks without fault and does what is right; he who tells the truth in his heart; he who works no deceit with his tongue; he who does no wrong to his neighbour; he who does not slander his neighbour.' 'He who casts the wicked devil, even as he beguiles him, out of the sight of his heart, along with the temptation itself, and so reduces him to impotence, and takes the incipient thoughts that he suggests and dashes them against (the rock of) Christ'; those who fear the Lord and do not become conceited about keeping the law well, but realise that the good in themselves cannot be their own work but is done by the Lord, and who praise the Lord working within them, as they say with the prophet, 'Not unto us, Lord, not unto us, but unto your name, give the glory.' For neither did the Apostle Paul give himself any credit for his preaching, but said, 'By the grace of God I am what I am.' And the same Apostle also said, 'He who boasts must boast in the Lord.'

&

Benedict encourages a prayerful and positive attitude to ourselves, others and God. And this spiritually-positive attitude is expected to blossom into good works. Again Benedict echoes the New Testament as he likens the spiritual life to running for a prize (1 Cor. 9.24; Heb. 12.1). Doing good deeds is our way of running towards the Kingdom, and, like running a race, doing good requires discipline.

The person who wishes to run in the Benedictine way should focus on three aspects of goodness. First, he should control his relationships: 'telling the truth in his heart, working no deceit with his tongue and never doing wrong to his neighbour'. Secondly, he will seek to gain mastery over his thoughts and inner desires. In a vivid and powerful image Benedict tells us to take our sinful thoughts and dash them against the rock of Christ. Finally, and most importantly, anyone who is seeking to live the righteous life must see that they will never succeed without the constant empowering grace of Christ (1 Cor. 15.10).

This wisdom is vital not only for our own spiritual lives, but also for the balanced formation of our children's characters. In a world where there is increasing pressure on children to succeed academically, socially and financially, Benedict's wisdom puts things in perspective. We must indeed try our very hardest to run the race and win the prize. But we must also understand that the ultimate success or failure rests not in our own efforts, but in God's grace. The final decision rests with him. Our business is to do our best – and let God do the rest.

This attitude not only gives God the glory (Ps. 115.1), but it relieves us from undue stress and worry. A proper understanding of how we co-operate with God grants us the dignity of real action and involvement while granting God the ultimate providence and power in our lives. This arrangement also teaches that God's love for us is unconditional. It does not rest on our success or fall by our failure.

Finally, a right understanding of our co-action with God also makes our Christian deeds eternally good because they are not the fruit of our own finite goodness: they are the actions of God becoming incarnate through our actions of love, in our family, our workplace and in our world.

THE PROLOGUE (E)

And so the Lord also says in the Gospel, 'Everyone who listens to these words of mine and acts on them, will be like a sensible man who built his house on rock; floods rose, gales blew and hurled themselves against that house, and it did not fall; it was founded on rock.' Thus the Lord concludes his reply, and daily expects us to respond through our dutiful actions to his holy precepts.

Therefore in order that amends be made for sins, the days of our life are prolonged to give us a time in which to make our peace, as the Apostle says, 'Do you realise that the patience of God is meant to lead you to repentance?' For this loving Lord says, 'I do not wish the death of the sinner, but that he should change his ways and live.'

❧

The Benedictine monk vows to pursue stability of life, and the need for stability is a constant theme throughout the Rule. Benedict himself lived in times of great upheaval. In the year 410 – just seventy years before Benedict's birth – the city of Rome fell to the invading hoards of barbarians, and by the middle of the century Huns were ravaging northern Italy. At the same time the Church was torn apart not only by the social and political chaos, but also by internal theological controversy.

His times are similar to our own. We have lived in a century of unparalleled violence, social upheaval, and cataclysmic change. Nothing seems secure and our whole world sometimes seems built on quicksand. In the midst of this our own lives too often shudder with insecurity, uncertainty and the stress of rapid transition.

So Benedict's injunction for us to build our house upon the rock is all the more timely (Matt. 7.25). Benedict teaches that the way to build sensibly on the rock is to obey the Lord's precepts and build carefully day by day – not attempting great things overnight, but constructing an edifice of faith which will withstand the tempests of life.

One of the greatest gifts we can give our children is a stable home life. We usually think only in terms of financial stability, but that is perhaps the least of our worries; in many ways finances will look after themselves. What is most often neglected is spiritual and moral stability. Christian values were once strongly supported by society, education and the media. But increasingly the Christian values that provide a stable home for our family seem like an outdated counter-culture.

Nevertheless, it is a strong and loving discipline of prayer, duty, and worship which provides not only the most stable environment for our homes, but also gives the surest foundation for our children to step out into the wider world with confidence.

This domestic stability can only exist if it is first being built in our own lives. There are various practical ways of building stability. With the help of a spiritual director we can put together a rule of life which gives form and structure to our spiritual quest. In today's reading Benedict provides the other plank in the platform of a spiritually stable life. He encourages repentance because it is through an attitude of repentance that we continually correct and modify our straying path.

THE PROLOGUE (F)

We have asked the Lord, my brothers, about the kind of man who dwells in his house, and we have heard what is required in order to do so. So let us fulfil the task of such a dweller. That means that we must make ready our hearts and bodies to engage in the warfare of holy obedience to his commands, and because our nature has not power to do this, we must ask God to send forth the help of his grace to our aid. And, if we wish to escape the punishment of hell and reach eternal life, then while there is still time, while we are still in this body and this life gives us the light to do all these things, we must hurry to do now what will profit us for ever.

☙

The Prologue to Benedict's Rule is full of loving encouragement and gentle enthusiasm. But it is also full of straight talking. In today's reading Benedict makes it clear that he is calling us to spiritual warfare and that we had better take him seriously if we wish to escape the pains of hell. The spiritual quest is not an option for people 'who like that sort of thing'. Our soul's destiny is at stake and time is short.

This is the uncompromising language of one who speaks with authority. We are unused to such language because the concept of authority has been eroded in our society. A cynical, questioning and rebellious attitude has become not only fashionable, but expected. The idea that we submit ourselves to a greater authority is shocking to most modern people, yet this is exactly what is required if we are to achieve stability and prosper spiritually. So Benedict makes no mistake when he likens his disciples to spiritual warriors. Like any soldier they must learn to take orders. And if a soldier must take orders, the commanding officer must take the greater responsibility of giving orders well.

In our age fathers are experiencing a crisis because their traditionally authoritarian role has been undermined. If the wrong kind of authoritarianism has been eroded, that may be a creative step forward. However, for the family to be secure the father still needs to exercise authority in the right way.

Christian authority is always shared in a vertical manner. Authority comes down from God through Christ to those with whom he shares his authority. In the Church his authority is shared with the successors of the apostles – the bishops. In the home God's authority is given to the parents since God has already shared with them the work and joy of the creative act. So as God gave Adam dominion over creation (Gen. 2.15), so God gives the man dominion within the family.

As Benedict does in today's reading, the one who holds authority must sometimes speak and act with firmness. While there is no call for the abbot or father to be tyrannical there is also no room for him to be pusillanimous. There are surely some men who err on the side of being too strict and dictatorial, but many more make the mistake of being too weak, lazy and complacent. For our homes to prosper men need to take up their God-given authority as fathers. We need to do so with maturity and humility, with good humour and without apology.

THE PROLOGUE (G)

*We propose, therefore to establish a school of the Lord's service,
and in setting it up we hope we shall lay down nothing that is
harsh or hard to bear. But if for adequate reason, for the correction of faults or the preservation of charity, some degree of
restraint is laid down, do not then and there be overcome with
terror, and run away from the way of salvation, for its beginning
must needs be difficult. On the contrary, through the continual
practice of monastic observance and the life of faith, our hearts
are opened wide, and the way of God's commandments is run in
a sweetness of love that is beyond words. Let us then never with-
draw from discipleship to him, but persevering in his teachings
in the monastery till death, let us share the sufferings of Christ
through patience, and so deserve also to share in his kingdom.*

If Benedict was firm in yesterday's reading, then in
today's passage he shows his gentler nature. In fact, the
stricter portions of the Rule are lifted from earlier monastic rules which served as Benedict's sources. Today's
reading, with its surge of tenderness and joy, is Benedict's
own. Here he shows how the authority of a Christian
father is properly expressed.

He does not wish to lay down anything 'too harsh or
burdensome', and Benedict is even at pains to explain that
the strict rules that do exist are there 'for the correction of
faults or the preservation of charity'. In the previous
passage Benedict may have warned solemnly of the pains

of hell, but here he uses a carrot, not a stick, to encourage his child in faith. If he perseveres he will 'run in the way of God's commandments with a sweetness of love that is beyond expression'.

So God's primary way of working is to draw us with the infinite delight of his love. Instead of the fear of hell, Benedict calls us to run in the way of God's commandments because that is what is best for us. Some discipline will be required, but that is because we are being summoned to grow up and become all that God intended, and to share in the highest and best gifts of his creation (Eph. 4.13). To quote Julian of Norwich: 'He loves us and enjoys us, and so he wills that we love him and enjoy him and firmly trust him; and all shall be well.'

The role of the Christian father is to reflect this kind of divine love to his children, so that in growing to love him they will be learning to love their heavenly Father as well. This will require discipline, but that discipline is always a servant to the higher law of love. Great wisdom is also required if we are to reflect God's love to our family. To do this Benedict will show us in his own gentle and humble way the wisdom necessary to fulfil this vocation. But he will also always remind us that 'we must ask God to send forth the help of his grace to our aid'. Then as the love of Christ is poured into our hearts (Rom. 5.5) we will be empowered to minister that love to those whom God has entrusted to our care.

CHAPTER I
THE KINDS OF MONK (A)

It is clear that there are four kinds of monk.
The first kind are the Cenobites, that is the 'monastery' kind,
who do battle under a Rule and an Abbot.
Then the second kind are the Anchorites or Hermits; these are
they who are no longer in the first fervour of their religious life
but have been tested for a long time in the monastery and have
learnt, with the assistance of many brothers, how to do battle
against the devil, and now, well equipped to leave the fraternal
battle-line for the solitary combat of the desert, they are strong
enough to do battle against the vices of the body and the mind on
their own, with their own resources, relying on God's aid, but
now without the support of anyone else.

༄

In outlining four types of monks, Benedict is also pointing
out four basic types of Christian. His aim is to encourage
cenobitic monks, those who live in an established community in obedience to an abbot. As such he addresses all
who live in an established community, whether it is the
nuclear family, or some wider community.

He gives pride of place to the solitary monks who fight
the spiritual battle single-handed. But he wisely observes
that no one should adopt this life until they have proved
themselves through a long life in a religious community.

While Benedict recognizes the high calling of the true
solitary he also understands that 'it is not good for man to
be alone' (Gen. 2.18). Benedict recognizes that being part

of a 'body' is integral to the Christian commitment (1 Cor. 12.27). In a society where more and more people are living alone, Benedict's call to community life encourages us to be 'joiners' and to get involved in our local communities.

The root of the word 'commitment' and the word 'community' is the same. It means 'with'. Benedict recognizes that the spiritual way is not easy and so calls us to run the path of perfection with others. In this way there is mutual support, faithfulness and loyalty. So the mature Christian will see the need to commit to others: first to his immediate family, then to his extended family, his local church, his workplace and his wider community. It is through his commitment to the monastic community that the monk grows spiritually, and it is through our commitment to our various communities that we learn the lessons of self-sacrificial love and construct stability in our lives.

It is important that children learn the value of commitment at an early age. This means a sense of duty should be taught from the beginning. The obnoxious wail, 'But that's boring!' ought to be checked at its first appearance. At that point even a young child should begin to accept that certain duties may not always be entertaining, and that commitment means being faithful in small things (Matt. 25.21). This is especially true of worship. Nothing has eroded the dignity of Christian worship more than the expectation that it must be entertaining. Regular attendance at church may not be entertaining, but that unfailing commitment establishes priorities and sets inner values that help build character and equip each child to face life's challenges with confidence.

CHAPTER I
THE KINDS OF MONK (B)

*The third kind of monk is the abominable one of Sarabaites, who
have not been tested by a rule, as gold is tested in a furnace, nor
been taught by experience, but are like soft lead. They keep faith
with this world by their actions, but manifestly lie to God by
their tonsure. These people live in twos and threes, or even
alone; they have no shepherd, they shut themselves up in their
own sheepfolds, not those of the Lord; and their law consists in
yielding to their desires: what they like or choose they call holy,
and they reckon illicit whatever displeases them.*

*The fourth kind of monk are those called Wanderers. These are
never stable throughout their whole lives but wanderers through
diverse regions, receiving hospitality in the monastic cells of
others for three or four days at a time. Always roving and never
settling, they follow their own wills, enslaved by the attractions
of gluttony. They are in all respects worse than the Sarabaites.*

*It is better to pass over in silence than to speak further of the
unhappy way of life of all these people, so let us pass them by,
and with God's help set about organising the strongest kind of
monks – the Cenobites.*

✌

Benedict discusses the four types of monk in order to high-
light the beauty and wisdom of the cenobitic life – the religious life lived within the confines of a monastic
community. In doing so he also exposes some problems
with two other approaches to religion and life generally.

To be a good Catholic is to be cenobitic. The cenobite

submits to a greater authority and lives in a community of obedience with those who share his authority structure. The sarabaite, on the other hand, is one who sets up shop on his own. There are many sarabaitic Christians. They determine what their authority structure is, and as Benedict points out, too often 'what they like or choose they call holy, and they reckon illicit whatever displeases them'. Sarabaitic Christians reject the teaching authority of the Church. They interpret Scripture according to their own needs, and the necessities of their age. Such a relativistic approach to the Christian life can only be ephemeral and ultimately destructive.

Benedict also recognizes the temptation to be a religious wanderer. For these 'gyrovagues' Benedict reserves the most scorn. The sarabaite Christians set up shop according to their own insights and opinions, but the gyrovague doesn't even have the courage or conviction to do that. Instead he wanders from one religious community to another like a bored goat. For him the grass is always greener on the other side of the monastic enclosure. He is thus destined to be constantly discontented, and subsequently to become a disgruntled complainer.

Similarly, in our consumer society it is all too easy for Christians to go 'church shopping'. With their own set of standards, they wander from church to church looking for the perfect community, the right music, the best priest. Such Christians not only never settle, but they usually cause trouble wherever they go. When a Christian father takes his family church shopping he subtly teaches them several untruths. First, that they are the final arbiters of which is the best church. Secondly, if they can choose from the different churches, then all churches are equally true. Finally, if they choose by personal preference they conclude that the form of worship is more important than the content.

Instead Benedict teaches that we learn everything through loyalty to the community we have been given. We should neither set up on our own nor wander about looking for the ideal life. It is our job to 'bloom where we are planted'. We should work to change for the better what can be changed, and to endure what cannot be changed.

CHAPTER II
WHAT KIND OF MAN THE ABBOT SHOULD BE (A)

An Abbot who is worthy to be in charge of a monastery must always bear in mind what he is called and fulfil in his actions the name of one who is called greater. For he is believed to act in the place of Christ in the monastery, since he is called by his title, as the Apostle says, 'You have received the Spirit of adoption as sons, through whom we cry, Abba! Father!' Therefore the Abbot should not teach or ordain or command anything that lies outside the Lord's commands, far from it; but his commands and his teaching should mingle like the leaven of divine justice in the mind of his disciples. The Abbot must always remember that at the fearful judgement of God two things will be discussed: his own teaching and the obedience of his disciples. The Abbot must also realise that whatever lack of fruitfulness the Father of the family may find in his sheep will be blamed on the shepherd. And likewise if the shepherd has laboured with complete diligence over a troublesome and disobedient flock, and has expended every care over their diseased behaviour, he will be acquitted in the Lord's judgement and will say with the prophet, 'I have not hidden your justice in my heart, but I have spoken of your truth and saving help'; 'but they have contemptuously despised me.' And then finally the penalty of death will swallow up the sheep who were disobedient to his care.

✎

The word 'abbot' means 'father'. The word shares the same

root as the Aramaic word *abba* – an especially intimate term like 'Papa' which Jesus himself uses for the Father (Mark 14.36), and which St Paul says we should use for God (Rom. 8.15). In his consideration of the traits of a good abbot or father this basic word *abba*, with all its implications of both intimacy and respect, comes into play.

In the monastery the abbot holds the rank of a bishop and, as the bishop holds apostolic authority, so Benedict is clear that the abbot's authority comes from Christ himself. In this he echoes the first-century writer, Ignatius of Antioch, who said, 'Clearly then we should regard the bishop as the Lord himself ...' Likewise the Christian father exercises authority in the family as from the Lord. St Paul commands children to 'obey their parents in the Lord' (Eph. 6.1–2), and thus keep the fourth commandment.

Anyone who glories in their position of power is a fool. Benedict recognizes that holding such authority over others is an awesome responsibility. The responsibility to speak and act as Christ in our families is a high calling which both lifts us up and casts us down at the same time. It lifts us up because we share in Christ's own ministry of reconciliation within our families (2 Cor. 5.18). It casts us down because we cannot 'speak Christ' if we don't 'live Christ'; and how can we hope to live Christ when we are aware that nothing good lives in us? (Rom. 7.18). Benedict then casts us down further when he says that we will be held responsible for the failure of our children.

How can any father hope to fulfil such a high calling? Benedict hints at the answer in today's passage. 'The abbot should not teach or ordain or command anything that lies outside the Lord's commands ...' In other words, the Christian father must clothe himself in Christ (Gal. 3.27) if he wishes to speak and live Christ in the home. This calls for a mysterious transaction in which we die to ourselves and live to Christ (Gal. 2.20). St Paul says this death to self is a daily requirement, and he grounds his own authority in this same identification with Christ (1 Cor. 15.31). Like-

25

wise a daily death to self is the only basis for a Christian father's authority in the home because it is through taking up our cross daily that we identify most fully with the Christ we hope to represent (Luke 9.23).

CHAPTER II
WHAT KIND OF MAN THE ABBOT SHOULD BE (B)

When, therefore, anyone takes the name of Abbot, he should rule over his disciples with two kinds of teaching; that is to say, he must show forth all good and holy things by his words and even more by his deeds.To apt disciples he must explain the Lord's teaching by word, but to those who are hard of heart or simple of mind he must make clear the divine teaching by his actions. By his deeds he must make it clear that nothing may be done which he has taught his disciples to be forbidden, lest while he preaches to others he should merit rejection himself, and God should some day say to him as he sins, 'What business have you reciting my statutes, standing there mouthing my covenant, since you detest my discipline, and thrust my words behind you?' And 'you observed the splinter in your brother's eye, and did not notice the plank in your own?'

∾

In this simple passage Benedict reminds us that we teach by both word and deed, and that one cannot succeed without the other. Benedict is also wise to point out that one form of teaching may be better for one child than another. Some children will learn more easily by being told: others need actions. Both will be watching to see if our words and actions agree, and the sobering truth is that in the end they will do as we do, not as we say.

It is vital that our teaching is backed up by our actions

to avoid hypocrisy and give weight to the truth. But the need for words and actions to agree has a deeper reason, because no truth is ever valid unless it is acted on. Practising what we preach goes right to the heart of what we believe as Christians because as we practise the truth we 'enflesh' the truth and make it visible. Trying to live the truth means our faith is never just a matter of agreeing to the right dogma or giving intellectual assent to a system of belief. Instead, faith itself becomes a way of life, a living and dynamic force woven into our very existence.

This kind of 'enacted faith' also has a prophetic element. The Old Testament prophets not only spoke God's word, but they often preached directly from circumstances around them, and took certain dramatic and prophetic actions. So in the home every opportunity should be taken to join moral teaching with real-life situations. The rough and tumble of family life should provide the classroom for the soul's growth. So it isn't good enough simply to declare what is right and wrong and expect obedience, but time should be taken to explain the ramifications of wrongdoing, and why a certain thing is wrong: e.g. because it hurts people. In this way the truths of faith and morals are constantly being woven into the patterns and actions of everyday life.

CHAPTER II
WHAT KIND OF MAN THE ABBOT SHOULD BE (C)

The Abbot must not show personal preferences in his monastery. He must not be more loving to one than to another, unless he had found him to be more advanced in goods works or in obedience. A free-born man must not be put before one entering the monastery from slavery, unless some other reasonable cause exists. But if it seems to the Abbot that there is good reason for it, let him do so, and let him do the same about the rank of anyone. Otherwise let them keep their normal order. For whether we are slaves or freemen, we are all one in Christ, and serve on equal terms in the army of one Lord; 'for God has no favourites'. In regard to rank we find distinction in his eyes only if we are found humble and better than others in good works. Therefore the Abbot should show himself equally loving to all, and maintain discipline impartially according to the merits of each.

In his life of St Benedict, Gregory the Great tells us how the community at Monte Cassino was composed of men from many different races and social strata. In managing them Benedict gives the basic rule that there is to be no favouritism in the abbot's dealings with his monks. God has no favourites (Rom. 2.11) and neither must the loving *abba*. Each person has equal favour in God's eyes; whether slave or free we are all one in Christ (Gal. 3.28). But this equality does not mean everyone is identical.

The abbot must overlook social rank. A monk entering from slavery or from the nobility is to be treated the same. This sounds very modern and enlightened, but we shouldn't think Benedict's attitude is exactly the same as our modern ideas of equality. Too often when we speak of equality we assume the lowest common denominator and reduce every individual to that degrading standard. Modern equality often means nothing more than drab uniformity. Too often 'equality' really means no one is permitted to excel. When Benedict speaks of not having favourites he is not endorsing a society of mindless fashion clones.

Instead, each monk is to be treated with an equal amount of love and attention. One is not favoured, because all are favoured. The loving *abba* recognizes in each one of his charges a unique, precious child of God with a set of gifts and needs like no other. He has no favourites because they cannot be compared. Each one is different and requires a unique blend of attention and delight.

So it must be in the home. It is difficult not to favour one child over another. One may be blessed with a sweet and loving nature while another is troubled with a sour and disagreeable disposition. We need grace to see in each one a special challenge to our love. Often the most troublesome people are the most gifted. Can we see the hidden abilities and gifts within the troublesome child? Are we aware of the faults which may lie hidden under the sweet demeanour of that favourite? The wise and loving father looks beyond the outward appearance and treats each member of the family with a blend of discipline and love which is just right for them. This may be an impossible ideal to attain, but we must always aim for the target – even if we often miss.

CHAPTER II
WHAT KIND OF MAN THE ABBOT SHOULD BE (D)

In his teaching the Abbot should always observe the method of the Apostle, 'Employ arguments, appeals and rebukes.' He must behave differently at different times, sometimes using threats, sometimes encouragement. He must show the tough attitude of a master, and also the loving affection of a father. Thus he should sternly reprimand the undisciplined and unruly, but entreat the obedient, the meek and the patient to go forward in virtue; as for the careless and the scornful, we instruct him to rebuke and correct them. He should not pretend that he does not see the faults of offenders, but remember the danger overhanging Eli, priest of Shiloh and, as best he can, he should cut them out by the roots as soon as they begin to show themselves. He should correct upright and intelligent minds with verbal admonitions once or twice, but the shameless, the thick-skinned and the proud or disobedient, he should repress at the very beginning of their sinful ways with the corporal punishment of blows, bearing in mind what is written, 'The fool is not corrected by words,' and again, 'Strike your son with the rod and you will deliver his soul from death.'

Benedict encourages the kind of equality which treats everyone equally while recognizing that they are not the same. How to do this can be summed up in one sentence from today's reading: He [the abbot] must show the tough attitude of a master, and also the loving affection of a father'. He must behave differently at different times with 'arguments, appeals and rebukes (2 Tim. 4.2): he needs to use both threats and encouragement.

As usual, Benedict's advice is simple, profound and full of common sense. He will give more detail about monastic discipline in the so-called 'penal code' of chapters 21–30, but here Benedict lays down some important foundation principles. First of all the abbot understands that discipline is not primarily to maintain communal order, but to build character. He will therefore focus on the faults of the individual and root them out like noxious weeds. Secondly, he will do this as soon as possible lest they grow up into bad characteristics which dominate the personality and handicap the person's social, mental and spiritual progress. Finally, the type and amount of discipline should be appropriate for each person's unique personality.

To establish these basic principles of discipline in the home requires us to be disciplined ourselves. Firstly, if we understand that discipline is not just to maintain order but to build character, then we will sometimes have to discipline our children even if what they are doing is not particularly disruptive or naughty. It is also difficult to root out the fault at its first appearance since faults often first show themselves in ways that seem rather harmless or 'cute'. But failure to recognize the fault and do something about it doesn't solve the problem: it only delays it, giving the weed time to grow into a plant which is too deeply rooted to be pulled out at all. Furthermore, when we fail to treat our children's faults in the first instance with measured and mild discipline, we are more likely to be reduced at some later stage to the frustration, violence and anger which we will regret, and which will only serve to compound the child's fault with resentment and rebellion.

CHAPTER II
WHAT KIND OF MAN THE ABBOT SHOULD BE (E)

The Abbot should always bear in mind what he is; he should bear in mind what he is called; and let him realise that more is demanded of him to whom more is entrusted. He must realise also how difficult and arduous is the task he has undertaken, that of ruling souls and serving men of many different characters; one, indeed, to be encouraged, another to be rebuked, another persuaded, each according to his nature and intelligence. Thus he must adapt and fit himself to all, so that not only will he not lose any of the flock entrusted to him, but he will rejoice as his good flock increases.

❧

The abbot and the father must always remember who they are and what they are called. They are called 'father' because God has shared with them the power of creation and entrusted them with the care of eternal human souls. This is a high calling, and one which should never be underestimated. One of the problems with modern life is that people have lost a sense of vocation. So many men support their families with anonymous jobs in huge government departments or large corporations. There is constant pressure to produce small results which are subsumed into the larger product. There is little satisfaction; the only reward is financial, and because the job seems meaningless too many men seek meaning by racing after the promise of promotion or higher pay. But this is an empty pursuit.

Instead the vocation of fatherhood is the one area where modern men can reclaim a sense of meaning in life. This means making our job as father the highest priority in life after our dedication to God himself. If we heed Benedict's advice always to remember that we are fathers and to remember the calling God has given, then a sense of vocation and meaning will come flooding back into our lives.

This will also help our marriages. Women often complain of the drudgery of housekeeping and the loneliness of looking after the children all the time. But this complaint is not so much that the women must stay at home and look after the children, but that they feel they are doing so with no help, no encouragement and little interest from their husband. So, quite fairly, women look for an escape from the monotony and loneliness of being 'just a housewife'.

But if their husband's priorities shifted and they both placed their marriage and their parenting as the highest priority, many of the problems would be solved. You could sum it up by saying that a woman's place is in the home, only if the man's place is there too.

And if the *abba*'s first priority is his home and family, then Benedict also tells us more about how to handle the children in his care. The *abba* must become 'all things to all men' (1 Cor. 9.22), adapting himself and his style of training to each of his different children. This job is not easy. It requires confidence, and enough strength of character to be constantly growing and learning. Entering fully into the demands of fatherhood is precisely how that growth and learning can take place.

CHAPTER II
WHAT KIND OF MAN THE ABBOT SHOULD BE (F)

It is most important that he should not pay greater attention to transient earthly things that pass away, and so fail to recognise or underestimate the salvation of the souls entrusted to him. Let him always consider that it is souls that he has undertaken to rule, and for whom he will give an account. Moreover, in order that he may not complain of reduced temporal goods, let him remember the Scripture, 'Seek God's Kingdom first, and his righteousness, and all these other things will be given you as well,' and again, 'Nothing is lacking to those who fear him.' Let him realise that he who undertakes to rule souls must prepare himself to give an account. Whatever the number of brethren under his care, he must understand clearly that he will have to render an account on the Day of Judgement for all these souls, in addition, of course, to his own. Thus as he bears ever in mind the enquiry that will be made on the shepherd's care of the sheep entrusted to him, the thought that he takes concerning the accounts to be rendered for others will make him careful of his own state. And so, while he provides by his instructions for the amendment of others, he will be brought also to the amendment of his own faults.

If we really make the health of our marriage and family our first priority we will soon be faced with some difficult decisions. The race for more money or greater business success will invariably take us away from home more. A promotion may mean moving house at a time when the children are settling well into their school and community. So putting the family first may require the sacrifice of our career, or a real reduction or limitation to our income.

Benedict again exhorts us to get our priorities right, no matter what the cost. We are not to pay more attention to 'transient earthly things that pass away [2 Cor. 4.18] and so fail to recognize or underestimate the salvation of the souls entrusted to [us]'. This is a great demand. Would we really be willing to refuse a promotion, accept a reduction in pay or even face redundancy in order to put our family first? These are real possibilities which we face in an increasingly competitive workplace.

Benedict's world was also financially insecure. So while he echoes the Lord's question, 'What does it profit a man to gain the whole world and lose his soul?' he also reassures us that the one who puts God's Kingdom first will have everything else added to him (Matt. 6.33). The promise is true that nothing is lacking for those who fear him (Ps. 33[34].10). One of the things to remember when weighing up priorities and commitments is that the sooner we decide that we have 'enough', the sooner we will be freed to do what we really want and ought to do.

It is possible to live a simpler life. It is possible to live as we ought to live and rely on God to provide our needs, and nothing will impress the faith on children more than seeing their own parents living sacrificially and trying to put their faith into action.

This is why Benedict reminds us that we will one day face a judgement where our actions and decisions will be weighed (Heb. 13.17). Because of this we are called again to make our families the very highest priority. We should do so because in helping to amend the lives of those in our care, we see our own faults more clearly, and so prepare ourselves for that day when our own lives will be judged (Rev. 20.12; Matt. 16.27).

CHAPTER III
ON SUMMONING THE BRETHREN TO COUNCIL (A)

Whenever anything important has to be done in the monastery the Abbot must assemble the whole community and explain what is under consideration. When he has heard the counsel of the brethren, he should give it consideration and then take what seems to him the best course. The reason why we say that all should be called to council is this: It is often to a younger brother that the Lord reveals the best course. But the brethren must give their counsel submissively and humbly and not presume stubbornly to defend their opinions. The decision should, however, depend mainly on the Abbot's judgement, and all should be joined in obedience to what he considers the soundest course. But just as it is fitting that disciples should obey their master, so it is incumbent on him to settle everything with foresight and justice.

◈

Jesus did not establish a republic, but a Kingdom. So the monastery, the Christian home and the Church are not democracies. When there is an important decision to be taken Benedict expects the abbot to summon the brethren not for a vote, but for consultation. The Latin word here is *consilium* not *concilium* – counsel not council. The abbot is to listen and consult, but in the end he bears the authority so he makes the decision.

Benedict's advice is balanced and wise. There are two

temptations in communal living: one, to let the leader take all responsibility, and the other, to let committees and elections take all the responsibility. Neither extreme works well. In the first the majority have no say, and in the second they have all the say. The first is wrong because one person is never always right and the second is wrong because the crowd is never always right.

So Benedict establishes a balance in which the clear authority of the abbot is balanced with consultation and genuine listening to the needs and opinions of all the brothers. It is especially interesting that the youngest of the brothers should also be listened to, for God often speaks through the mouth of the youngest since they have a special wisdom and purity which is linked with their youth and inexperience.

So likewise a Christian family is neither a dictatorship of the father nor a democracy of the mob. Instead the father and mother have absolute authority in the home, but that authority is exercised for the good of the children. They may not often be summoned for a formal family meeting, but the good father and mother will listen to the children and be sensitive to their needs at all times.

Listening attentively to our children is the best and most natural form of consultation. Listening to them is difficult because their conversation is often banal and repetitious. But in granting them full attention we construct a regular form of consultation and maintain open channels of communication which are invaluable. With this kind of listening, parents will be able to settle everything with justice and foresight. Furthermore, the time spent listening to our toddlers will pay off later because we will find we have open and loving teenagers instead of sullen, silent ones.

CHAPTER III
ON SUMMONING THE BRETHREN TO COUNCIL (B)

In every circumstance, therefore, all should follow the authority of the Rule, nor is it to be rashly abandoned by anyone. No one in the monastery is to follow the prompting of his own heart; no one is to presume to argue rudely with the Abbot, or to argue at all outside the monastery. If anyone does so presume, he must submit to disciplinary measures. The Abbot himself, however, in all his actions must fear God and keep the Rule, bearing in mind that most surely he will have to render account for all his decisions before God, the most just judge.

If, however, there are less important matters to be transacted for the well-being of the monastery, the Abbot should take counsel only with the senior monks, for it is written, 'Take counsel about all you do and afterwards you will have no regrets.'

&

There are two points which apply to family life in today's reading. Firstly, Benedict makes it clear that the abbot is subject to the Rule just as the monks are. So children, like monks under obedience to an abbot, will find it far easier to obey if they see that their parents also follow the rules.

Having clear rules of behaviour for everyone in the home is the best way to encourage harmony and peace. Everyone likes to know where they stand and what is expected of them – especially children. Within this chapter which encourages consultation, it is good to remember that rules should be established together in a family. St Paul advises us not to embitter our children (Col. 3.21). Nothing irritates more than having rules imposed arbitrarily. So while children should learn to obey unconditionally, it is also fair to explain why the rules are there and how everyone benefits from them. Likewise the system of rewards and sanctions should be discussed and explained fairly. It is far easier to obey when we know exactly what the consequences of our action will be.

Keeping to the rules not only helps children, but it helps us as well. If we take the time to explain the rules, rewards and sanctions, then we will understand better what we hope to achieve. We will also be less likely to lose control and punish harshly if we observe a fair system of warnings and positive rewards which we have established together.

Benedict's second point concerns the proper way to argue within the family. Notice that Benedict doesn't forbid argument. Instead he lays down some rules. So children should be forbidden from arguing with parents outside the home. This is not only an unsociable display of bad temper, but it shows disloyalty. Within the home disagreement is allowed, but the monk should never 'argue rudely' with the abbot. Somehow in family quarrels we have to express our anger without falling into uncontrolled rage and violence. We also have to avoid the error of bottling up our emotions and responding with supercilious superiority.

The usual reason that argument becomes either heated or icy is because a problem has been brewing for some time and no one has had the courage to bring it into the open. So the best way to keep argument manageable is to encourage constant and open communication. Both children and parents should be able to express their feelings honestly, but without losing control. Of course things sometimes become nasty. That's how we learn to wrestle with the dragon of our emotions. The remedy is not to forbid harsh words, but to struggle together to put things right with instant forgiveness, and the resolution to do better next time.

CHAPTER IV
THE TOOLS OF GOOD WORKS (A)

In the first place to love the Lord God with all one's heart, with all one's soul and with all one's strength.

Then to love one's neighbour as oneself
Then not to kill
Not to commit adultery
Not to steal
Not to covet
Not to bear false witness
To honour all men
Not to do to another what one would not wish to have done to oneself
To deny oneself in order to follow Christ
To punish one's body
Not to seek pleasures
To love fasting
To relieve the poor
To clothe the naked
To visit the sick
To bury the dead
To give help in trouble
To console the sorrowful
To avoid worldly behaviour
To set nothing before the love of Christ

This chapter is full of riches, and four lifetimes would be too short to plumb its depths, much less four days. Like all of Benedict's Rule, chapter four reads like common sense, but on closer reading we see a deep inner logic. We see how it is imbued with Scripture, and how its simple wisdom flows from a profound understanding of God's grace working within and through the complexities of human nature.

The first part of the chapter can be broken down into two sections. The first opens with two general rules: Jesus' summary of the law to love God and our neighbour (Matt. 22.37–39; Mark 12.30–31; Luke 10.27). Then flowing from this are the commands not to injure others by killing, stealing, coveting, and lying. The section is summed up with two other general rules: to honour everyone (1 Pet. 2.17), and to treat others as we wish to be treated (Tobit 4.16; Matt. 7.12; Luke 6.31).

The second part of the reading has to do with self-control. It starts with this verse: 'To deny oneself in order to follow Christ'. So we should discipline the body. And the later verse which reads 'Not to seek pleasures' has been charmingly translated by Catherine Wybourne as, 'Not to hug good things to oneself'. Finally, we exercise self-control with fasting. The practice of fasting is a discipline which opens windows of the soul. Just one aspect of the benefit of fasting is a greater identification with those in need. So we are called to minister to the physical and emotional needs of others before being reminded to 'set nothing before the love of Christ'.

This is no mere list of do's and dont's. Instead the order of the list shows us not only what to do, but how to do it and why to do it. The first part of the list gives us a high command to love God and our neighbour. We do this by learning self-control. The monk disciplines himself physically in order to learn inner control. The fruit of this self-control is the active love of others, and eventually the ability to 'set nothing before the love of Christ'.

The family gives us the context to use these 'tools of

good works'. We have to share, we have to get up in the middle of the night for a crying infant. We have to sacrifice ourselves to support our family. In addition, the family is a unit which can administer these virtues in the world. Together the family can reach out to others and minister God's love, so fulfilling Christ's twofold command to love God and our neighbour – remembering that in our needy neighbour Christ himself is found (Matt. 25.31–46).

January 19
May 20
September 19

CHAPTER IV
THE TOOLS OF GOOD WORKS (B)

Not to give way to anger
Not to cherish an opportunity for displaying one's anger
Not to preserve deceit in one's heart
Not to give the kiss of peace insincerely
Not to abandon charity
Not to swear, for fear of perjury
To speak with one's mouth the truth that lies in one's heart
Not to return evil for evil
Not to inflict any injury, but to suffer injuries patiently
To love one's enemies
Not to curse anyone who curses us, but instead to return a blessing
To suffer persecution for righteousness' sake
Not to be arrogant
Not given to drinking
Not a heavy eater
Not given to much sleeping
Not lazy
Not a grumbler
Not a detractor
To rest one's hope in God
Whenever one perceives any good in oneself to attribute it to God, not to one's self
But to recognise that whatever is evil is one's own doing, and to blame one's self

This section of chapter IV can also be split into two smaller parts. The first part helps us deal with anger towards others and the second part directs our attention to the fruit of unexpressed anger in our lives.

Once again Benedict does not forbid anger. But he advises how to control it. We mustn't give in to anger or nurture an opportunity to 'tell someone off'. We mustn't harbour a lie in our hearts or pretend to like someone when we don't. Instead we are to speak honestly and openly with everyone, never return evil for evil (1 Thess. 5.15), or curse for curse. We must bear injuries patiently (1 Pet. 3.9; Matt. 5.10) and love our enemies (Luke 6.27).

But too often anger remains unexpressed. When it festers in our minds the rot soon sets in. Our souls become infected and if we are not careful our whole lives can be destroyed. So the second set of commands considers the effects of unexpressed anger. How is unresolved anger manifested in our lives? – the list is here. We become arrogant, we seek escape and solace in too much food, drink and sleep. Then we grumble, backbite and snipe at others.

Instead of harbouring anger like this, Benedict advises us to look at ourselves clearly. We need to acknowledge that any good in us is God's doing, while any evil is our own responsibility. These are hard words, and nothing goes against the grain more than to give up nursing anger and acknowledge that the problem is probably with us.

It is vital within our marriage and family to sort out the problem of anger as soon as possible. Many relationships are founded on a brooding anger which grows from false expectations. The only way to cure the demon of anger is to confront it head on, to bring it out into the open and get things right, and the only one who can put it right is God.

Psychologists tell us fear lies at the root of anger. At the very foundation of our personalities we are angry because we are frightened. This is the inchoate fear of the child being left alone in the dark, cut off from love. The only remedy for this underlying fear is that deep unconditional perfect love (1 John 4.18) which can only be found in God himself. So Benedict ends this section on inner problems by advising us to 'rest one's hope in God', for in him alone will we find the healing love which drives out anger and fear.

CHAPTER IV
THE TOOLS OF GOOD WORKS (C)

To fear the Day of Judgement
To dread hell
To yearn for eternal life with all possible spiritual desire
To keep death daily before one's eyes
At every moment to keep watch over the actions of one's life
In every place to know that God most surely beholds one
To dash the evil thoughts that invade one's heart immediately upon Christ, as upon a rock, and to reveal them to one's spiritual father
To guard one's mouth against evil and vicious speech
Not to love much talking
Not to utter words that are foolish and provoke laughter
Not to love much or unrestrained laughter
To listen willingly to devout reading
To fall often to prayer
In our daily prayer to God to confess with tears and groans the wrong-doing in our past life
To amend these wrong ways in the future
To reject carnal desires
To hate one's own will
To obey the Abbot's commands in everything, even though he himself (which God forbid) acts otherwise, remembering always that command of the Lord's, 'Do what they tell you, but do not do the things that they do'

*To be unwilling to be called holy before one is so, but to be
holy first so that it may be truly said of one*

The first part of this chapter sets out the basic toolkit of
good works. The second considers the different aspects of
anger. Today's portion deals further with the inner life.
Once again, it can be split into two parts. The first encourages us to face our own mortality and the inevitability of
judgement. It can be summed up by the verse: 'To keep
death daily before one's eyes'. The second dimension to
the inner life deals with our thoughts and words.

Benedict reminds us that we shall all surely die, and
that hell remains a real possibility, for even the holiest
person may be tempted to commit mortal sin. So we are to
keep watch over every action and thought. This is important because we often excuse in our thought-life such
things as we would never excuse should they be acted out.
The Scripture is clear about the destructiveness of lust
(Prov. 6.25) and St Paul says lustful thoughts and
covetousness are idols (Col. 3.5). Jesus also tells us not to
give in to lust (Matt. 5.28).

Benedict recommends a creative treatment for evil
thoughts: take them and mentally dash them to pieces on
the rock which is Jesus Christ, then tell them to your
confessor. This is actually a very dynamic and positive
way to deal with evil thoughts. If we ignore them they
keep nagging at us; if we try to suppress them they only
get stronger. Evil thoughts are a corruption of the imagination, so we should use the same faculty – the imagination – to visualize those idols being smashed on the rock of
Christ.

The second part of today's reading focuses on the other
part of our inner life – our words. The monk is not only to
avoid speaking evil of others, but he should also avoid too
much foolish talk and unrestrained laughter. This is not to
say that we should stifle our sense of humour. Instead
Benedict is rightly pointing out that senseless chatter and
constant raucous laughter is the mark of a superficial

person. Furthermore, linked with the earlier verses, Benedict understands that more often than not ceaseless chatter and laughter is either at the expense of others or it is coarse and shallow. The first is cruel, the second is empty.

The remedy for sinful thoughts is prayer and the cure for sinful words is good reading. In the home this simply means we should make the effort to keep our minds and tongues engaged in positive activities so we occupy the very parts of us which, when lying idle, can so easily turn to evil.

CHAPTER IV
THE TOOLS OF GOOD WORKS (D)

To carry out God's commands daily in one's actions
To love chastity
To hate no one
Not to cherish bitterness
Not to indulge in envy
Not to love quarelling
To flee vainglory
To revere the elders
To love the young
To pray for one's enemies in the love of Christ
After a quarrel to make peace with the other before sunset
And never to despair of God's mercy
These then are the tools of the spiritual craft. If we make full use of them unceasingly day and night, then, when we give them back on the Day of Judgement, we shall in return receive from the Lord that reward which he himself has promised, 'The things that no eye has seen, and no ear has heard, which God has prepared for those who love him.' Now the workshop in which we make diligent use of all these tools is the enclosure of the monastery combined with stability in the community.

❧

Benedict concludes his inventory of the toolkit of good works not by giving more commands, but by pointing to the sort of person we are meant to become in obeying his commands.

So Benedict encourages his monks to love chastity rather than to take a vow of chastity. Chastity is not the same thing as celibacy. Celibacy means sexual abstinence, whereas chastity means sexual faithfulness. Therefore, chastity is a virtue for all Christians, single and married. Benedict implies that chastity is more than sexual self-control, however. Chastity means purity or simplicity, so in recommending that we 'love chastity' Benedict means we should not only avoid impurity (Col. 3.5) but we should also become a pure person, putting on the new self (Col. 3.10; Eph. 4.22–24), and becoming pure in heart (Matt. 5.8).

The one who is pure in heart will, by God's grace, be able to follow the rest of Benedict's commands to hate no one, not to cherish bitterness nor indulge in envy, and to flee arrogance. He sums up the attitude of the pure soul by recognizing that they will love young people, revere the old and pray for their enemies in the sincere love of Christ.

Almost as an afterthought Benedict reminds his monks of Eph. 4.26: that one should not let the sun set on a quarrel. This is excellent advice for any marriage and family. Before turning out the lights every family member should be at peace with one another. By morning the grievance may seem forgotten, but if the problem hasn't been put right it will only have gone deeper, to fester and poison the relationship later. In chapter thirteen Benedict gives a good suggestion to put things right. Recite the Lord's Prayer together. No family quarrel will last long when the two parties say together, 'Forgive us our sins as we forgive those who sin against us'.

Finally, Benedict encourages us in the use of these tools of perfection by reminding us never to despair of God's mercy. We may try our best and fail repeatedly, but God is always there to make up the deficit, restore us to our feet and give us the strength to run 'in the path of his commandments with inexpressible delight of love'.

CHAPTER V
OBEDIENCE (A)

The first step in humility is prompt obedience. This is fitting for those who hold nothing more dear to them than Christ. Because they had made profession of holy service or for fear of hell or to attain the glory of everlasting life, immediately when something has been commanded by a superior, it is for them as a divine command and they cannot allow any delay in its execution. The Lord says of them, 'As soon as he heard me, he obeyed me.' And he said also to those who are to teach, 'Whoever listens to you listens to me.'

Such men, therefore, at once leave whatever they are engaged on, abandon their own will, and with hands set free by leaving unfinished what they are doing, with the quick feet of obedience, follow by action the voice of him who gives the order. And so it is as if in a single moment the order of the master is uttered and the work of the disciple is completed with the speed inspired by the fear of the Lord. The two things are swiftly completed together by those in whose hearts lies the desire of reaching eternal life. Thus they take the narrow way, as the Lord says, 'Narrow is the way that leads to life.' So they do not live according to their own wills, nor obey their own desires and pleasures, but behaving in accordance with the rule and judgement of another, they live in monasteries and desire to have an Abbot ruling over them. Without doubt such men imitate the mind of the Lord in his saying, 'I came to do not my own will, but that of him who sent me.'

Our entire culture conditions us to seek our own will. Consumerism encourages us to be self-indulgent. Educational theory teaches us to be sceptical and not to believe until we have tested something ourselves. Individualism tells us to 'express ourselves', and hedonism encourages us to seek our own pleasures first. Protestantism allows us to seek the church which gives us most pleasure, and some moral teachers say our individual conscience is the sole test of right and wrong. In the midst of this culture Benedict's uncompromising call for obedience is radically subversive.

Furthermore, he requires his monks to obey immediately because the abbot speaks in the place of the Lord himself (Luke 10.16). This is a prompt, military-like obedience – dropping everything at once to obey the command almost before it is spoken. This sort of person really does follow the narrow way that leads to life (Matt. 7.13–14).

But if Benedict is so adamant that obedience is necessary, he makes clear why this is so in the first sentence of today's reading. Prompt obedience is the first step in humility. If that is so, then it is clear that those who have no masters but themselves have not even begun to acquire humility. The other reason why obedience is vital is because we are here to acquire the mind of Christ who came to do God's will (John 6.38) and became obedient even to death (Phil. 2.5–8).

If Christ was so obedient, then our whole Christian journey must begin with obedience. Those in authority over us in the Church speak with the voice of Christ himself (Luke 10.16; 2 Pet. 3.2). This doesn't mean that obedience is easy. The Church's teaching is tough. Complete obedience is almost impossible. That's why it's called the narrow way. Nevertheless, this is the mountain we are given to climb. This is the path in which we are called to run.

If we, as fathers, take the call to obedience seriously then we will always be sensitive to the difficulty our children have in learning to obey. We will also be careful to explain our requests as much as possible, and endeavour never to lay on them anything which is too much of a burden, remembering that while they are called to obey us, we are also commanded not to exasperate them, but to bring them up in the training and instruction of the Lord (Eph. 6.4–5).

CHAPTER V
OBEDIENCE (B)

This obedience of which we speak will be acceptable to God and agreeable to men if what is ordered is carried out without fearfulness, without slowness in performance, without half-heartedness or grumbling or an unwilling reply. For the obedience that is shown to superiors is shown to God; for he said himself, 'He who listens to you, listens to me.' And it should be offered by the disciples with good will, because 'God loves a cheerful giver.' For if a disciple obeys grudgingly, if he complains not only in words but even in thought, then, although he carries out the order it will not now be acceptable to God, who sees that his heart is grumbling; and for work like this he will get no reward – indeed, he incurs the penalty for grumblers, unless he make amends with penance.

☙

Benedict not only calls for obedience, but for cheerful obedience because 'God loves a cheerful giver' (2 Cor. 9.7). To obey grudgingly is better than to disobey, but to obey cheerfully shows a truly humble heart. The importance of obedience to spiritual maturity cannot be overestimated, because obedience in spirit is at the heart of a truly Christ-like attitude (Php 2.5–8).

If we think about it, we soon see that obedience isn't really so unusual. Every day we are required to obey a whole host of forces greater than ourselves. We must submit to the law, our health, our climate, our economy, our employer. In fact, there are more things in life beyond our control than within our control. At any moment some calamity may strike us or we may be caught up in the machinations of another person's will.

This does not mean that the Christian is meant to be a doormat or a fatalist. Active obedience is not the same thing as passive submission, nor is the acceptance of authority acceptance of powerlessness. We are commanded to take action and to make a difference in the world: obedience simply means it is God's will and not our own which we are seeking to enact. So the essence of obedience lies in the prayer, 'Not my will, but thy will be done on earth as it is in heaven' (Matt. 26.39; Matt. 6.10).

This prayer takes us to the heart not only of Jesus' own prayer life, but also to the heart of his experience in Gethsemane. It reminds us that our life is meant to be hid with Christ in God (Col. 3.3). This hiddenness has been acclaimed and lived by all the saints and it is the essence of obedience.

If cheerful obedience is necessary for our own spiritual growth, then it is also a necessary foundation for strong Christian character in our children. We are not being unfair when we expect them not only to obey, but to do so cheerfully. Of course there will be absurd moments when the 'cheerfulness' is forced. The best thing to do in that case is to recognize the hilarity of the situation, and without being unkind, help them to see the funny side and be reconciled through the gift of laughter. That not only defuses the problem; it also prompts the desired cheerfulness – even if it is in a roundabout way.

CHAPTER VI
ON KEEPING SILENCE

Let us do what the prophet says, 'I have resolved: I will watch how I behave and not let my tongue lead me into sin; I set a muzzle over my mouth; I stayed dumb, I was humbled, I refrained from speaking even good words.' Here the prophet teaches that if we should sometimes for the sake of the virtue of silence refrain even from good conversation, we should all the more, for fear of the penalty of sin, refrain from evil words. Therefore, because of the great importance of keeping silence, permission to speak should be rarely given even to exemplary disciples, for conversation that is good and holy and edifying; for it is written, 'If you talk a lot you will not escape falling into sin,' and elsewhere, 'Death and life are in the power of the tongue.' Indeed it is fitting for the master to speak and teach; the disciple's part is to keep silent and to listen.

Therefore, if it is necessary to ask a superior for something, the request should be made with humility and submissive reverence. But as for loose talk, idle words and talk that stimulates laughter, we condemn this with a permanent ban in all places, and we do not allow a disciple to open his mouth in this kind of speech.

❧

Benedict here advises strict limits on conversation, realizing that the tongue is a deadly member of the body which can lead to terrible evil (Jas. 3.6–8). In addition Benedict even recommends not saying good things, lest in starting to talk we end up being led into evil. But Benedict's warnings against too much talk are not just warnings against frivolous chatter and gossip.

His main reason for telling us to be quiet is because 'the disciple's part is to keep silent and to listen'. Remember the root of the word *obey* is 'to listen' and Benedict opens the Rule with his call, 'Listen my son ...'. We are called to listen not only to the commands of our masters, but most of all to the word of God which comes to us through the Scriptures, and the 'still small voice' of the Spirit (1 Kings 19.12). We are to be silent therefore in order to hear the Word of the Lord, and to enter into the communion of silent love with him. We are to carry this silent communion in our hearts at all times. This can only be done if we first keep a guard on our own lips, and seek to cultivate an environment of silence in our lives.

Our modern life militates against silence of any kind. In addition to the roar of traffic, aircraft and crowds, we are bombarded with radio, television, electronic bleeping and ubiquitous shallow music. Furthermore, there is a kind of printed noise pollution in which we are besieged by mountains of written drivel in the form of advertisements, newspapers and magazines. If we are not careful, our minds and those of our family are swamped, and there isn't the tiniest bit of time to nurture inner silence.

It is vital to control the noise element in our homes. Television and radio should be turned off more than on: just as Benedict says we don't have to say a good thing, so, even if there is a television programme worth watching, it doesn't mean we must watch it. On a positive note, we should also encourage times of silence within the home for each child. Within family prayers there should be silence. Church should be a place of silence. It is a creative and positive thing for each child to have a 'quiet place' where they can be still, curl up with a book and begin to find within themselves that inner ear which can learn to be attuned to the 'still small voice' of the Spirit.

CHAPTER VII
HUMILITY (A)

Brothers, Holy Scripture cries aloud to us, saying, 'Whoever exalts himself will be humbled, and he who humbles himself will be exalted.' When it says this it is teaching that all exaltation is a kind of pride. And the prophet shows that he himself was on his guard against it, when he said, 'Lord, my heart has no lofty ambitions, my eyes do not look too high; I am not concerned with great affairs, or marvels beyond my scope.' Why thus? 'If I did not think humbly, but exalted my soul, as a child on the mother's breast is weaned, so did you treat my soul.'

Financial and social success is the aim of most people and a raft of self-help books encourage us to promote ourselves with self-confidence, or the 'power of positive thinking'. In the face of this 'dress for success' mentality, humility seems an embarrassingly poor garment. And yet humility is central to the Christian way of life, and this chapter on humility is at the heart of St Benedict's teaching.

We think grovelling is humility. We also mistake modesty or self-deprecation for humility. But none of these represent true humility. For Benedict humility is linked with self-knowledge. The truly humble person is the prodigal son, who gets to the very bottom of his resources, where, as the Authorized Version puts it, he 'comes to himself' (Luke 15.17) and realizes his need of the father's love. This kind of self-knowledge does not grovel before others. Nor does it indulge in maudlin self-pity or overblown guilt. Instead it is a clear, hard and realistic self-appraisal.

Benedict rightly points out that humility is the core virtue because it is the opposite of pride; and it is pride which destroys community, destroys families and finally destroys the soul. So he quotes the Lord's words that whoever exalts himself will be humbled, while he who humbles himself will be exalted (Luke 18.14). And he likens the humble soul to the little child who simply relies on his mother (Ps. 131). This is reminiscent of Mother Julian's words: 'Full lovingly does our Lord hold us when it seems to us we are nearly forsaken and cast away because of our sin ...' and Julian emphasizes God's tenderness when she affirms, 'As truly as God is our Father so just as truly he is our Mother'.

It is this utter reliance on God's love which gives Christian humility an inner dignity. This is the blend which St Paul talks about when he says we should boast not of ourselves, but of the Lord (2 Cor. 10.17). This is the same combination which we must seek to nurture in our children. As they grow we should develop with them a clear understanding of their strengths and their faults. This lucid self-knowledge will then provide the basis for the proper sort of 'self-confidence' – a self-confidence which is not arrogant and proud, but an honest blend of personal humility and confidence in the father's powerful and undying love.

CHAPTER VII
HUMILITY (B)

So, brothers, if we wish to reach the highest peak of humility, and to arrive quickly at that state of heavenly exaltation which is attained in the present life through humility, then that ladder which appeared to Jacob in his dream, on which he saw angels going up and down, must be set up, so that we may mount by our own actions. Certainly that going down and up is to be understood by us in the sense that we go down through pride and up through humility. The ladder itself that is set up is our life in this world, and the setting up is effected by the Lord in the humbled heart. The sides of the ladder we call the body and soul, and in them the divine call inserts the diverse rungs of humility and (interior) discipline.

Benedict outlines a twelve-point plan for acquiring humility. In doing so he likens spiritual growth to Jacob's ladder (Gen. 28.12). The sides of the ladder are body and soul and the rungs are the various steps of humility. Paradoxically, to ascend the ladder we must go down in humility, while going up in pride means descending the ladder.

So Benedict puts his twelve steps of humility in a tidy and logical sequence. However, the picture of a ladder cannot be pressed too far. An earlier monastic writer, John Cassian, says the different degrees or steps are like different signs or indications of humility. We mustn't think that one step follows another in chronological order. Instead the different 'traits of humility' may come in any order and they must all exist together.

It is important to remember that in all things strict formulas rarely work. They are only guidelines for behaviour and planning. So in bringing up our children we cannot force each one into a watertight plan for the successful formation of character. Instead we must have an overall view and work day by day to help each one develop his gifts and overcome his faults as the opportunity arises.

There is one thing which is challenging about Benedict's teaching. He actually thinks we can make progress in acquiring humility. This too cuts against the grain of our modern mindset because we often give in to a kind of fatalism. We excuse sin by pointing to our upbringing, our circumstances or the fact that 'we're only human, after all'. This is a kind of twisted pride which refuses to take responsibility for our thoughts and actions. In laying out a twelve-point plan for acquiring humility Benedict once more encourages us to take responsibility for ourselves and to seek our soul's salvation while there is time.

Finally, if the way of humility is like Jacob's ladder, then the way of ascent is only through Christ himself. In John 1.51 Jesus says that Nathaniel will 'see heaven opened and the angels of God ascending and descending on the Son of Man': so he alludes to Jacob's vision, but likens himself to the ladder of ascent, for he is the only bridge between God and man (1 Tim. 2.5), and it is only through identification with his humility that we can hope to learn humility ourselves.

CHAPTER VII
HUMILITY (C)

The first step of humility, then, is for a man to set the fear of God always before his eyes, and utterly to avoid forgetfulness. He must always remember all God's commandments, and constantly turn over in his heart how hell will burn those who despise him by their sins, and how eternal life has been prepared for those who fear him. At every moment a man must be on his guard against sins and vices – vices of thought, word, hand, foot or self-will, and also against the desires of the flesh. He must recognise that he is at every hour in the sight of God in heaven, and that his actions are everywhere visible to the divine eyes of God, and are being reported to God by the angels from moment to moment. This is made clear to us by the prophet when he shows us that God is always present in our thoughts, 'God examines', he says, 'the heart and the mind.' And also, 'The Lord knows exactly how men think.' And yet again, 'You read my thoughts from far away' and 'Even the thought of man shall praise you.' In order then to keep his perverse thoughts under careful control, the profitable brother should repeat in his heart, 'Then I shall be spotless in his sight, if I keep myself in check against my sinfulness.'

❧

The first step of humility is to keep the fear of God before our eyes. Benedict reminds us that God is not only omnipresent, but he knows every thought and desire of our hearts (Pss. 7.9; 94.11). We must therefore be conscious of every action and thought and work out our salvation with fear and trembling (Phil. 2.12).

Nowadays we are attracted to a cosy heavenly Father, and reject the idea that we should fear God in any way. But the Scriptures say the fear of God is the beginning of wisdom (Prov. 1.7) and it is the wicked man who has no fear of God (Ps. 36.1). Benedict paints God as a fearsome judge and warns his disciples of the pains of hell. How are we to reconcile ourselves to such an unfashionable viewpoint?

Relationships within our own natural families shed light on our relationship with God the Father. Psychologists tell us that for the infant the mother is the source of warmth, nourishment and life itself. The father is the great 'Other'. While the mother is the subjective source of comfort the father is the objective source of authority. The infant has an instinct of fear towards life in general and it is natural for this inchoate fear to be focused in the father first of all.

But perfect love casts out fear (1 John 4.18) so we must grow into a realization that our father loves and cares for us. Adolescent rebellion is often only the child's natural instinct to throw off the rules of the fearsome father in order to discover the real loving person behind the rules. If we can understand this process we will be able to help it along and not imprison the child in an immature stage of development. The final stage of the father–child relationship is where both relate in the loving and responsible freedom of adults.

The same stages are required in our relationship with God. As Benedict teaches, we rightly start with fear of God. We move on to a relationship of obedience based on fear – a relationship out of which many people never advance. But we must move on, most often through some crisis which reflects adolescence – a crisis which drives us away from God. This needs to be followed by a mature relationship of love and freedom, a joyful relationship pictured in the return of the prodigal son (Luke 15.24). So the deepest love for God develops not out of sentimentality, but out of the basic instinct of fear, and unless that fear is acknowledged we will never develop that more mature love.

CHAPTER VII
HUMILITY (D)

Scripture, indeed, forbids us to do our own will, saying to us, 'Turn away from your will.' Moreover, we ask God in our prayers that his will may be done in us. Truly then we are taught not to do our own will, when we accept the warning of Scripture, 'There are ways which seem right to a man, but in the end they plunge him into the depth of hell,' and also when we tremble at what is said of the indifferent, 'They are corrupt and depraved in their pleasures.' Indeed in what concerns the desires of the flesh, we must believe that God is ever present to us, even as the prophet says, 'All my desires are known to you.'

Benedict quotes plenty of Scripture to remind us of the perils of putting our will before God's. We are to turn away from our own will (Sir. 18.30), and pray that God's will may be done in our lives (Matt. 6.10). Benedict is certainly criticizing those who are completely indifferent to the ways of God, but not many of them will be in the monastery, so he is probably really attacking the sarabaitic view of Christian life.

In the opening chapter he explained that the sarabaites were those monks who lived according to their own will: 'What they like or choose they call holy, and they reckon illicit whatever displeases them'. These are not so much the ones who do evil, but those who do what seems good in their own eyes. Benedict considers such individualism to be deadly for the soul, and he supports it by quoting

Proverbs 16.25: 'There are ways which seem right to a man, but in the end they plunge him into the depth of hell'.

Going it alone in the spiritual life is deadly for several reasons. Firstly, it is dangerous because it leads to complacency. Presumption is the sin in which we believe we have made it spiritually when we haven't even begun the journey. But spiritual self-determinism also leads to trouble because we have no objective criteria for judging the state of our own soul. Our motives are so mixed and our self-analysis so biased that we simply cannot know if we are going in the right direction. The soul is a vast country. We need guides and maps to make our journey or we soon get lost, and this confusion can lead finally to despair and loss of faith.

Our children reflect our own profound lack of self-knowledge. The four-year-old who cries, 'But I'm not tired!' as her eyes are drooping, or the seventeen-year-old who is trying out an absurd new 'look' are both cut off from their true selves. We are not much different if we think we can walk in the way of Christ with no guide but our own desires, ideas and conscience. Just as they need the loving, humorous, objective voice of the father to see themselves, so we need a spiritual father to enlighten and guide us.

CHAPTER VII
HUMILITY (E)

We must, therefore, be on our guard against any evil desire, because death is stationed beside the entrance to delight, as Scripture teaches in the words, 'Do not go after your lusts.' So if the eyes of the Lord are upon the good and the wicked and if the Lord is always looking down from heaven upon the children of men to see if there are any that act wisely and seek after God, and if daily our works are reported to the Lord by the angels assigned to us, then brethren, we must constantly be on our guard, lest one day God beholds us falling into sin and becoming unprofitable and (although he spare us in this life because he is merciful and waits for our repentance) he should say to us in the hereafter, 'This you did, and I was silent.'

✧

The first step of humility is to keep the fear of God before our eyes, and here Benedict keeps reminding us that the eyes of the Lord are on all of us (Prov. 15.3), looking down to see who is acting justly (Ps. 14.2). In this passage Benedict deals with the particular form of self-will called lust, quoting from Scripture that we should not 'go after our lusts' (Sir. 18.30).

Lust is the indulgence of improper sexual desire. But the sin of lust goes far deeper than simply impure thoughts and fantasies. Dante makes it clear that the problem with lust is that it is a perversion of love. What God has given to teach us self-giving, lust twists into selfish desire. So the destructive power of lust lies not in sex itself, but in the self-centred perversion of sex.

Not only is pornography freely available in our society, but advertising and the modern mass media constantly fuel the roaring fire of lust. Everywhere we are bombarded with images of impossibly beautiful young men and women who look as if they are seething with lust. So the advertisers link the volcano of sexual desire to our desire for almost everything else, and we cannot even choose a tub of ice-cream without lust being linked in to entice us. This constant barrage of lustful images twists our corporate view of sexuality and makes lust seem like the norm rather than the perversion.

In such a context how can a Christian family hope to obey Benedict's command not to follow after our lusts? The main remedy is for an open and honest attitude to sex in the home. Modesty and chastity do not have to be synonymous with suppression and shame. When it is appropriate, sex should be discussed seriously and openly with each child. A major part of the father's role is to affirm each child's sexuality. In her relationship to her father a girl learns to be a woman, and it is the father who shows the boys how to be men. From the beginning sexual matters should be put into perspective; then when the time is right children can be taught to understand God's healthy role for sexual relationships within marriage. When that is put right they might just see the shallow foolishness of the lustful world for what it is. In this context humour and honesty is worth far more than secrets and shame.

CHAPTER VII
HUMILITY (F)

The second step of humility is that a man should not love his own will nor take pleasure in carrying out his desires, but rather by his actions imitate the Lord in his saying, 'I came not to do my own will, but that of him who sent me.' And it has been written, 'Self-indulgence brings its penalty, endurance brings forth a crown.'

The second step of humility is linked with the first. The first is to keep the fear of God before our eyes, while the second is a logical follow-on from that. If we are constantly aware of the presence of God then we will wish to submit our will to his in every moment. In cultivating this attitude we are imitating Christ who came not to do his own will, but the will of the one who sent him (John 6.38).

This is not easy because our first instinct is always self-preservation, self-pleasure and self-will. How can we begin the elemental shift which puts the will of God before our own? Once more the key lies in obedience-listening. Obedience springs from listening, and listening is a form of obedience. The art of listening to God and listening to others is incompatible with self-will, and listening to God and listening to others is linked because we cannot love God if we will not love our neighbour.

To listen intently therefore is an action of attentive love. This attentiveness is not only due when our loved ones speak to us, but we should be attentive to their needs at all times. We need to listen to what our wives and children are saying, but we also need to listen to what they are *not* saying. Listening intently is not only an activity of our ears. Real listening means being sensitive to their moods and paying attention to their inner agenda. This requires attention to body language, tone of voice, facial expressions and those eloquent silences within relationships.

So good listeners listen with their eyes, their hearts and their emotions. Real listening means understanding and developing sympathy. Real listening means getting into another's circumstances and seeking to understand their deepest needs. Real listening is a skill which requires discipline and hard work. But it is vital to do this work because we must root out self-will, and it is impossible to listen to another person completely and remain self-centred.

This total listening leads to love, because as we come to understand a person better we can accept him or her unconditionally. Christian love is not feeling fond of someone all the time, but being willing to understand and accept them as they are. Listening-obedience is the way the loving father submits to his children. They need the attentive love and we need to give it, not only for them, but also for the sake of our own souls.

CHAPTER VII
HUMILITY (G)

The third step of humility is that for the love of God one should be obedient to a superior in all things, imitating the Lord of whom the Apostle says, 'He was made obedient even unto death.'

❧

The third step of humility puts flesh on the second step. The second step advises us to put away self-will. We actively do this when we obey a superior in all things. Benedict reminds us again that this is what Jesus did. He 'did not cling to equality with God, but took the form of a servant and became obedient even unto death' (Phil. 2.8).

Benedict cannot hammer home the importance of obedience enough. He sees clearly that every act of obedience should be an act of love. Every act of obedience is another nail in the coffin of our pride and self-will. Every act of obedience is a death to self and a living to someone else and to God. Every act of obedience is an act of service. Every act of obedience is therefore an act of humility, and every act of humility takes us further into the mind of Christ.

Within the home we expect our children to obey us. We may even expect our wives to obey us. Wives submitting to husbands seems terribly unfashionable, but is there any reason why women should not be allowed the challenge of obedience? In fact the Scripture commands both of these forms of obedience within the family (Col. 3.18–20; 1 Pet. 3.1, 5–6).

But in calling wives to obedience St Paul doesn't condone dictatorial husbands. According to the biblical principle, the husband and father, like Benedict's abbot, stands in the place of Christ in the home (Eph. 5.22–24). As such he leads the way in self-sacrifice. So the husband and father is to lay down his life for his wife and family just as Christ loved the Church and gave himself for her (Eph. 5.25). St Paul says this is how we imitate Christ. In Benedict's terms the wife obeys her superior – her husband. At the same time the husband lays down his life for his superior – his wife.

This is not the mastery of one person over another, but the total and mutual self-sacrifice which should be the foundation of any Christian marriage and community. This is a high ideal, but we shouldn't scrap the ideal because some people have twisted it to their own ends or because we fail to keep it. Instead we should proclaim the ideal clearly and do our best to fulfil it with God's help.

CHAPTER VII
HUMILITY (H)

The fourth step of humility is that, when in the very act of obeying one meets with trials, opposition, and even abuse, a man should, with an uncomplaining spirit, keep a firm grip on patience and as he endures he should neither grow faint nor run away; even as Scripture says, 'He who stands firm to the end will be saved,' and again, 'Let your heart take courage and hope in the Lord.' Further, to show us how a faithful man should suffer all things, however painful, on the Lord's behalf, it gives voice to those who suffer in the words, 'For your sake we are afflicted by death all the day long, and are reckoned as sheep for slaughter.' Yet unmoved, through their hope of divine reward they joyfully persevere, saying, 'These are the trials through which we triumph on account of him who has loved us.' And elsewhere Scripture says again, 'You tested us, O God; you refined us in the fire as silver is refined; you led us into the net; you laid tribulations on our backs.' And to show that we ought to be under a superior, it continues, 'You have set men over our heads.' Precisely then they patiently fulfil the command of the Lord in these trials and rebuffs, and when they are struck on one cheek they offer the other. When someone takes away their tunic they allow him to take their cloak also. When they are forced to go one mile, they go two; like the Apostle Paul they put up with false brethren, and bless those who curse them.

❦

Benedict's fourth step of humility tells us what to do when acceptance becomes almost overwhelmingly difficult.

Submission to our lot in life is a form of obedience which Benedict encourages unreservedly. So this reading has much to say about our attitude to our marriage and family.

There must be very few men and women who, at some point in their marriage, didn't want to get out. We talk of the marriage bond, and that's exactly what it is: binding. If we take our marriage and family seriously then the responsibilities infringe on our personal wishes and plans. When the pressure becomes too great we naturally want an escape, and suddenly an affair or divorce becomes a seductive alternative.

But Benedict doesn't allow that option. When faced with the gruelling work of community life he says we should 'keep a firm grip in patience', neither growing faint nor seeking an easy escape route. Benedict has made it clear that obedience is the narrow way, and that running away from our problems doesn't solve anything.

Instead Benedict recommends fortitude and patience. These are old-fashioned virtues, strengths that seem absurd in a world where everyone is hell bent on gaining the next ephemeral pleasure no matter what the cost. And yet Benedict piles up Scripture after Scripture to support his case that we must endure the suffering which comes to us in life. For he who stands firm to the end will be saved (Matt. 10.22), and although we suffer, these are the trials through which we triumph (Rom. 8.36–37). They are the fire in which we are purified (Ps. 66.10–11).

The lifelong marriage vow is just as serious as the monk's solemn vow. Equivalent hardships are demanded of the Christian married man as of the Christian monk. Equivalent sacrifices are expected, and equivalent joy and rewards may be gained. When we endure the difficult times of family life and struggle through them to a resolution we are setting the best example possible for our children. They know instinctively that life has its hardships; they are watching to learn from us how to deal with them. And if we persevere, they will learn that giving up never wins, that running away accomplishes nothing and that patience carries you through. On a deeper level, embracing our hardships is not only the crucible of our refinement: it is also an intimate meeting point with Christ.

CHAPTER VII
HUMILITY (I)

The fifth step of humility is that a man should in humble confession reveal to his Abbot all the evil thoughts that come into his mind, and any wrongful actions that he had done in secret. In this connection Scripture exhorts us in the words, 'Reveal your course to the Lord, and hope in him,' and again, 'Make confession to the Lord for he is good, and his mercy is everlasting;' and yet again the prophet says, 'I have declared my sin to you, I have not covered up my evil actions; I made this resolve: I will confess my evil deeds to the Lord, and you have forgiven the guilt of my heart.'

❧

We often forget what a beautiful and powerful gift we have within the sacrament of reconciliation. To make an honest, open and humble confession is one of the speediest ways to experience an outpouring of God's grace in our lives. Of course confession is humbling. Repentance is not easy, but through sacramental confession we humble ourselves under the mighty hand of God that he may lift us up. In confession we cast all our cares on him who cares for us (1 Pet. 5.6–7).

Personal sacramental confession as we know it was not fully developed in Benedict's time. When Benedict recommends confession to the abbot, the relationship is more that of spiritual director than formal confessor. So it does us good to have a regular confessor who knows us and can guide us successfully in the spiritual way. Benedict says we should tell him our evil thoughts and the actions we have done in secret. The temptation is to take the easy route and simply 'tell God we're sorry' about the evil thoughts and shameful deeds. But Benedict is for having them out in the open. This is painful, but healthy. It is healthy spiritually because it leads to honesty and humility. But it is also healthy psychologically. Once a secret thought or deed is out in the open it ceases to be such a monster. In the light of the confessional it is put into perspective and any power it had to breed in the darkness of our souls is removed.

Our children should have the right image of the sacrament of penance. Too often the confessional looms in the imagination as a dark, forbidding and shameful place. This bad image is the work of the devil, and it is up to us to show our children that going to confession is a healthy, light-filled time of forgiveness and growth. They should see us going to confession regularly and regard it as a part of healthy family life.

Confession is also important for the spiritual development of the child because careful preparation for confession is the best way to instruct the conscience properly. It is also the best way to understand how sin alienates us from God and from one another. Finally, it is only through revealing our course to the Lord that we learn to hope in him (Ps. 37.5), and it is by making our confession to the Lord that we come to experience his everlasting mercy.

CHAPTER VII
HUMILITY (J)

The sixth step of humility is that a monk should be satisfied with whatever is of lowest value or quality, and with regard to the tasks laid on him should think of himself as a bad and unworthy workman, repeating to himself the words of the prophet, 'I have been brought to nothing; I have known nothing; I am like a pack-animal before you ... and yet I am always with you.'

❧

In the sixth step of humility Benedict says we should be satisfied with whatever is of the lowest value or quality. Furthermore, we should see ourselves as bad and unworthy workmen – just lowly pack-animals. This seems like artificial grovelling and an unnecessary asceticism. Why should we be content with things of poor quality and regard ourselves as unworthy workmen?

Benedict is not so much advising a false grovelling as calling us to take a realistic view of our work and our possessions. First of all we should be content with what material things we have. Benedict – unlike St Francis – does not embrace poverty for its own sake, but he does encourage us to be satisfied with things that are of poor quality if that is what we have. Not only should we be satisfied with these material things, but we should also learn not to judge by outward appearances. Rich material possessions don't save souls – just the reverse.

In advising us to see ourselves as unworthy workmen Benedict is probably referring to Luke 17.10 where Jesus says the servants who have done everything they have been told to do reply, 'We are unworthy servants, we have only done our duty'. This is therefore a double mark of humility: that we do not pride ourselves in our rich possessions or in our good works. This is important because these are the two areas of life where pride creeps in almost unseen. St John calls it the lust of the eyes and the pride of life (1 John 2.15–17).

While Benedict says we should be content with our possessions and regard ourselves as unworthy workmen, he does not say we should despise physical things or human accomplishment. Elsewhere he is clear that we should treat our possessions carefully as gifts from God and that we should value our work. His point here is simply that we are not to invest everything in our possessions or our work. These things are secondary to the service of God and the path of humility. Besides, both are gifts from God in the first place and should not be a cause for our pride.

We need to establish the right balance in our own view of work and possessions so our children will understand how these aspects of life fit into the whole. The sooner they learn to be content with what they have, and see their accomplishment as a gift from God the sooner they – and we – will experience real freedom.

CHAPTER VII
HUMILITY (K)

The seventh step of humility is that he should not only say in words that he is inferior and less virtuous than all other men, but that he should really believe it in the depth of his heart, making the same act of humility as the prophet, who says, 'I am a worm and no man; the scorn of mankind, the jest of the people.' 'I have been lifted up, I have been brought down, and reduced to confusion.' And again, 'It is good for me that you have humiliated me, so that I may learn your commandments.'

❧

In his seventh step Benedict takes our self-abnegation to an even lower level. On first reading, this amount of abject humility almost seems comical. Surely so much grovelling is more like a form of twisted spiritual pride than real humility. He quotes Ps. 21.7: 'I am a worm and no man ...', and 'It is good for me that you have humiliated me, so that I may learn your commandments' (Ps. 119.71). This extreme humiliation might seem comical, but Benedict is making a serious point. He is challenging us to confront our own self-image.

This worm-talk sounds absurd and we would never use such language about ourselves. But haven't we used similarly degrading language about others? In fact we don't hesitate from using even worse language about others in their absence. So if we feel able to denigrate others, why not ourselves? In fact not only do we speak cruelly of others, but we usually do so in order to exalt ourselves in our own eyes. We put others down to make ourselves feel better.

Benedict advises us to do exactly the opposite. We put others down to exalt ourselves, but the humble man genuinely sees the best in other people, not the worst. He sees their potential. He sees the extenuating circumstances that cause their faults. He gives them the benefit of the doubt and a second chance. Because he sees the good in other people he also genuinely regards himself as 'inferior and less virtuous than all other men'.

Furthermore, as Benedict observes, the humble man is often reduced to confusion (Ps. 88.16). He knows how his inner life is a mass of contradictory emotions and motives. He knows how his faults sometimes seem like virtues and his virtues seem like selfishness. Unlike most of us who attempt to sort ourselves out, the humble man thanks God for the confusion and humiliation because it is a chance to trust him more (Ps. 119.71).

Such humility is a gift. We can't affect such humility by outward show, but we can work towards a transformation of our attitude to self and to others. We should nurture the ability to recognize the good in others and to understand the circumstances which led to their bad behaviour. Whenever possible we should help our children to understand why things have gone wrong in relationships and help to give them a second chance. We should also help them to recognize the good in one another and express it. This begins to build the habits of mind which may grow into the humility which Benedict recommends.

CHAPTER VII
HUMILITY (L)

The eighth step of humility is that a monk should do nothing except what is recommended by the common rule of the monastery and the example of those above him.

In his eighth step of humility, Benedict returns again to the need for us to submit ourselves to our surroundings and disciplines of our given life. As Thomas à Kempis writes, it is not up to us to change the world, but to change ourselves. So humility comes through fitting in, not by sticking out.

One of the most difficult things in the world is to keep our mouths shut when we think we know the answer. We may see the best way to do something or the answer to a particular problem, but it may not be our place to speak. We need then to fit in, be quiet and let those who are in authority take the decisions and solve the problems, even if they do it badly.

This grates. We want to be pro-active in the world. We want to take charge and make things happen, but we are not always in a position to do so. We may have moved to a new community, a new job, a new church. Others occupy the positions of leadership and authority that we are used to. In such situations we must keep quiet and listen. Being placed in a lowly position is hard on the ego. We all want to be somebody special. Sometimes we are tempted to achieve this by some mark of individualism or eccentricity like unusual dress or manners; but this is immature.

Fitting in is a discipline that leads to hiddenness. The greatest saints all speak of the hidden quality of their lives. They may have been in enclosed convents like Thérèse of Lisieux or they may have been active in the world, but they all speak of the hardship of learning to take second place and keep quiet, even when they knew what was best.

In the home it is vital that each child is allowed time to speak and express himself or herself. But it is also vital that they learn how to keep silent and listen, even when they think they know best – especially when they think they know best. This discipline is important for us too, because in fact we rarely know best. The way of a fool seems right to himself (Prov. 12.15), but even a fool is thought wise if he keeps silent (Prov. 17.28).

CHAPTER VII
HUMILITY (M)

*The ninth step of humility is that a monk should keep his tongue
from talking; he should preserve silence and not speak until he is
questioned, for the Scripture teaches that, 'In much talking, one
will not escape sin,' and that 'the talkative man is not directed
in his life.'*

In the next three steps of humility St Benedict once more
considers the role of silence. In the ninth step he reminds
us that 'in much talking one will not escape sin' (Prov.
10.19), and that 'the talkative man is not directed in his
life' (Ps. 140.11). Benedict simply recommends silence, and
leaves it at that. When we analyse our conversation we can
see the profound wisdom of his advice.

We should ask what we spend so much of our lives
talking about and who we are really talking to. If we are
honest an awful lot of our talk is to ourselves. We like to
hear ourselves talk. We like to hear our own opinions
tumbling forth. We like to win arguments and like laugh-
ing at our own jokes. Sadly what we call conversation is
often nothing more than one long self-congratulatory
stream of talk which we bounce off other people.

And what do we talk about? Don't we spend an awful
lot of time talking about ourselves? I'm my favourite topic
of conversation. I talk about my ideas, my clever plans, my
work and my arguments with people. So much of my talk
is not only to myself: it is also about myself. Benedict real-

izes that it is this constant self-centred talk which indicates a person with no direction. He has no object outside himself, no focus for his love and service. The person who talks constantly about himself lives in an ever-dwindling downward spiral. So Benedict recommends an outward discipline of silence which nurtures inner growth in humility.

Children naturally talk about themselves. While we need to listen to them talk about their exploits, we also need to control the conversation, allowing space for others to speak and encouraging each child to listen intently. This not only fosters their social skills, but it teaches them to curb their tendency to talk about themselves and so observe the silence which Benedict says lies at the core of the humble heart.

CHAPTER VII

HUMILITY (N)

The tenth step of humility is that he should not be ready and quick to laughter, for it is written, 'The fool raises his voice in laughter.'

❧

The tenth step of humility also deals with an outward sign of humility. We are not to be ready and quick to laugh. This seems harsh, but Benedict includes it at the end of this section on humility because he is showing that certain outward traits grow from the development of the inner humility. He is not so much prescribing action as describing the humble man's character.

So when he says we are not to be quick and ready to laugh Benedict is not forbidding laughter. Neither is he suppressing a natural sense of humour and fun. Instead he is simply observing that the humble soul is not forever looking for frivolous entertainment. The opposite of the humble person is the fool who is constantly on the lookout for the latest gag, silly trick or foolish game. This sort of fool uses humour as an escape from the serious questions. His instant humour is shallow, evasive and silly. It disturbs his own peace and the peace of others.

More sophisticated humour is often even more soul-destroying. If television comedy isn't crude, blasphemous and cruel, then it is simple, shallow and stupid. Such humour is often based on a secular nihilism which destroys everything with an air of distrust, bitterness and cynicism.

Benedict is not advocating glum faces. He would be the first to recognize and encourage real Christian joy. The truly humble person radiates a joy which inspires laughter, smiles and a supernatural happiness which is quite unlike the giggles, snorts and silliness which come from jokes, pranks and humour for their own sake. The person who is filled with joy sees the humour within our human condition and accepts the hilarity of life with a kind of innocence that is never cynical or cruel.

Children's humour, at least in their younger years, is usually quite innocent. It enjoys tickling, slapstick, pulling faces and funny word-games. We can relearn this innocent humour from them, and then as they grow older we have the opportunity to help them develop their humour to be rich and joyfully ridiculous without being cruel, crude or crass.

CHAPTER VII
HUMILITY (O)

The eleventh step of humility is that when a monk speaks, he does so quietly, without laughter, with humility, with restraint, making use of few words and reasonable ones, as it is written, 'The wise man becomes known for his few words.'

❧

In this final word about silence Benedict not only recommends what to speak – as few words as possible – but he also says how we should speak them: 'quietly'. Benedict gives this advice not only because silence is a virtue in itself, but because words are precious, and our language is always to be used wisely.

Jesus warns us that we will be held responsible for every idle word that comes from our mouth (Matt. 12.36). What we say has real power for good or evil. We must be careful how we speak to one another because that is how we communicate our feelings for them. It is through our words that we either build up or tear down. Nothing we say is neutral because all words have both a denotative meaning and a connotative meaning. That is, our words have face value, but they are spoken within an emotional context, and that unspoken message is often communicated more powerfully than the words themselves. So in our family relationships words become precious. They are the carriers of not only our thoughts, but also our feelings.

Not only are we to speak few words, but we are to speak them softly. But if Benedict encourages reticence and quietness, he does not encourage suppression of our emotions. In chapter three he allows argument and full discussion with all members of the community. So within the Christian family conversations should be controlled, quiet and honest. If we lose our temper and things descend to an undignified screaming match we have lost it and need to repent. It seems much easier to say, 'We are only human'. But that excuses us too easily. It overlooks the real hurt caused by lost tempers and pretends the damage doesn't matter.

In fact emotional violence is sometimes worse than physical violence because with physical violence we see the pain and physical injury. But with emotional violence the injury is internal and invisible. Emotional violence goes deep and inflicts permanent damage on the developing child. So within the family context Benedict's words are especially important. We need to make it a family policy that a soft answer turns away anger (Prov. 15.1), and be reminded of the teaching of St James: 'Everyone should be quick to listen, slow to speak and slow to anger' (Jas. 1.19).

CHAPTER VII
HUMILITY (P)

The twelfth step of humility is not only that a monk should be humble of heart, but also that in his appearance his humility should be apparent to those who see him.

That is to say: whether he is at the work of God, in the oratory, in the monastery, in the garden, on the road, in the field or anywhere else, whether sitting, walking or standing, he should always have his head bowed, his eyes fixed on the ground, and should at every moment be considering his guilt for his sins and thinking that he is even now being presented for the dread judgement. He should always be saying in his heart what the tax-gatherer in the Gospel said with downcast eyes, 'Lord, sinner as I am, I am not worthy to raise my eyes to heaven;' or again with the prophet, 'I am bowed down and humbled at all times.'

Thus when all these steps of humility have been climbed, the monk will soon reach that love of God which, being perfect, drives out all fear. Through this love all the practices which before he kept somewhat fearfully, he now beings to keep effortlessly and naturally and habitually, influenced now not by any fear of hell but by the force of long practice, and the very delight he experiences in virtue. These things the Lord, working through his Holy Spirit, will deign to show in his workman, when he has been purified from vice and sin.

☙

Benedict wants inner humility before there is any outward sign, knowing that any false outward gestures of humility will always be signs of pride instead. Nevertheless he advises that wherever we are, we should behave with a quiet demeanour. A monk never shows off. St Paul captures the same humble Christian spirit in some advice to the Thessalonians: 'Make it your ambition to lead a quiet life, to mind your own business and work with your hands' (1 Thess. 4.11). Benedict also says this quiet demeanour reflects the inner awareness of our sinfulness and need of God's mercy (Luke 18.13).

Then in a lyrical passage of hope Benedict completes his treatise on humility. All the steps of humility were motivated by the awareness of our sinfulness and fear of God's judgement. But Benedict encourages us to press past that to the point where the habits of humility become natural. What was done out of fear is now done out of love (1 John 4.18). As he says in the prologue, the disciple now 'runs on the path of God's commandments with the inexpressible delight of love'.

This work of grace does not elevate the Christian to some superhuman level of sanctity. Instead it makes him fully human. He is not given something alien to his nature: instead his humanity is restored to that fullness and constant fellowship with God from which he first fell. The saint who, by God's grace, achieves perfection is therefore the most natural of people. He is an example of all that a human being can and should be. He is in harmony with himself and with the whole universe. Living in constant communion with God the truly humble soul displays the fullness of human potential. This is the simple and pure glory for which God has called each one of us (Eph. 1.4).

As Benedict points out, this state of simple perfection is only attained by going through a profound awareness of our sinfulness and emerging from the trial purified. This purified soul enjoys a perfection greater than Adam's. Adam was perfect, but had never sinned. In Christ we can go through the darkness of sin and death to emerge triumphant. This complete victory over sin is a possibility for every Christian (1 John 5.4, 18). Running in the path of

St Benedict is one way, through God's grace, that we may attain it (2 Tim. 4.7–8). Even the glimmer of such a possibility should speed us on our way.

CHAPTER VIII
THE DIVINE OFFICE AT NIGHT

Having considered what is reasonable we lay down that during the winter (that is from 1 November till Easter) the time of rising will be the eighth hour of the night. Thus they may sleep for a while after midnight and get up after digestion has been completed. The time that is left after Matins is to be used for further study by the brethren whose knowledge of the Psalter or of the readings is incomplete. From Easter till the aforesaid 1 November, the hour of rising should be so determined that there is a short interval after Matins, during which the brethren can go out for the necessities of nature. Lauds which follow are to be said as dawn is breaking.

In the first part of the Rule Benedict lays down the foundation for our spiritual development. In chapters eight to twenty he specifies the rules and disciplines of monastic prayer. At first sight these sixth-century rules about how to order the monastic Office and how many psalms to sing seem irrelevant both to modern life and the administration of a Christian home.

But we should look again. In all the particular rules a certain Benedictine ethos is communicated. Benedict's unique blend of firm rules tempered with an understanding of human weakness shows us how to set up our own guidelines in the home. But, more importantly, the particular rules show how incarnational Benedict's Rule is. In chapter seven he stresses how much humility and holiness is learned by fitting in, buckling down and getting on with the ordinary disciplines and denial which daily life demands. By focusing on detail in this next section, Benedict reminds us that it is in the day-to-day routine, in the physical details of life, that holiness is to be found. In the Benedictine vision the most mundane elements of life are woven into the tapestry of prayer.

So in today's reading he blends earthy concerns about the monk's digestion and time for the lavatory into his rules about time spent singing the Office. He also tells us that the prayer of the monks is to synchronize with the seasons of the year and the time of day. Time is important for Benedict. Ordering time is a way of ordering life. In his day, the night began around six o'clock. So when he tells his monks to rise at the eighth hour that means they get up at two in the morning to sing the Office called Vigils or Matins. In the summer months when the days are longer they are to rise in darkness, have a short break after Matins, then welcome the dawn with the morning Office of Lauds.

Very few monks get up at two in the morning these days, whereas any father with little children is used to getting up in the small hours of the morning. It is easy to be disgruntled by the midnight demands of small children. Benedict would tell us to use that time for prayer. We may not be able to pray formally while walking a restless baby, but we can join in repetitive prayer like the rosary or the Jesus prayer. If the children are older we can always try to go to bed earlier so we can get up earlier. Praying while the sun rises is a joy anyone can share with a bit of discipline.

CHAPTER IX
THE NUMBER OF PSALMS TO BE SAID AT THE NIGHT OFFICE

During the winter period mentioned above, first of all there should be said three times the versicle, 'Lord open my lips, and my mouth will proclaim your praise,' to be followed by Psalm 3 and the Glory be; *after this Psalm 94 should be chanted with an antiphon, or at least chanted. Then the hymn should follow, and next, six Psalms with antiphons. When these are ended and the versicle has been said, the Abbot should pronounce a blessing. Then when all are seated in their stalls, three readings should be read by the brethren in turn from the book on the lectern, and between them three responsories should be sung. Two responsories should be sung without the* **Glory be**, *but after the third reading, the singer should chant the* **Glory be**, *and when he begins it all should at once rise from their seats in honour and reverence for the Holy Trinity. The books of divine authorship, of both the Old and New Testaments, should be read at Matins, and also the commentaries on them written by well-known and approved Catholic Fathers. After these readings with their responsories another six Psalms should follow; they are to be sung with Alleluia. After these Psalms, there should follow a reading from the Apostle, recited by heart, the versicle, and the prayer of the litany, that is* **Lord have mercy**. *And so let Matins conclude.*

❧

Chapter nine gives liturgical details about the night Office. This was a very important part of the prayer cycle for

Benedict, and he spends much time laying down guidelines for its correct procedure. The night Office is important because it sums up the monastic calling. It does so in several ways which also apply to us. In the night Office the monk wakes up to praise God. This reminds us of Benedict's command in the prologue to 'wake up' and live a life of awareness. But in waking up to praise God the monk also engages in battle with the forces of darkness. In Benedict's time the night was considered the time of evil, so in punctuating the night with prayer the monks engage the devil on his own territory. We need to be reminded that we are engaged in spiritual warfare (Eph. 6.12ff.). Finally, the night Office was probably said in darkness. It was a prayer of waiting, watching and listening. This too sums up the spiritual life, for often we pray in an inner darkness, waiting for God's answer to enlighten us (Ps. 88.1).

As he will do in the rest of this section of the Rule, Benedict stipulates which psalms should be said. The psalms are the bedrock of monastic prayer. They should be the foundation of our devotions as well. The reason the psalms are so important for Christian prayer is because in the psalms we do not have historical stories, apostolic letters or doctrinal teaching. Instead we have heartfelt personal prayers to God. The psalms encompass the whole range of human emotion from ecstatic joy to utter desolation. So the psalms too should be part of our individual and family prayer.

If we use a form of daily prayer of the Church, then psalms will form a large part of the liturgy. We should not only recite them, but try to memorize particular bits because Scripture memorization keeps us from sin (Ps. 119.11). The psalms should also be a cornerstone of our family prayers. There are simple musical versions of some psalms like 'The Lord is my Shepherd', Taizé chants or modern choruses which even very young children can learn. We should search them out and use them to nurture the language of prayer in the hearts and minds of our children. If memorized, the psalms will flower in their hearts and minds forever.

CHAPTER X

HOW THE PRAISE OF GOD IS TO BE PERFORMED ON SUMMER NIGHTS

From Easter till November the same number of Psalms, as set down above, is to be retained, but on account of the nights being short, no lessons are to be read from the book. Instead of these three readings, one from the Old Testament is to be recited by heart, followed by a short responsory. All the rest should be carried out as set down above. Thus, never less than twelve Psalms should be said at Matins, not counting the 3rd and 94th.

In the shorter nights of summer Benedict abbreviates the night Office. He does this for two practical reasons which reveal principles for Christian community. Benedict could shorten the hours of sleep, but he chooses to shorten Matins instead. So he obviously has no time for a legalism or asceticism which is so strict as to be destructive. He realizes that body, mind and spirit need to be alert and healthy in order to worship and work efficiently. This reminds us that we all have basic physical needs, and we shouldn't punish ourselves or our children by making unreasonable demands.

Benedict also shortens the night Office because Lauds is said at dawn and he wants to preserve a break between the two Offices. The principle is that we should order time – not allow it to order us. We need to understand the rhythms of each day and the differing needs of our family throughout the day. These practical concerns are important. They are not separate from the spiritual quest.

Within the home, therefore, we should be sensitive to the needs of our wives and children just as God provides for us (Matt. 7.9–11). Providing for them does not simply mean bringing home a pay cheque. But being aware of the needs of others isn't easy; our own insensitivity is compounded by the fact that very often we human beings don't know why we are unhappy. We imagine there is some terrible problem, when one practically-minded mother has observed that 95 per cent of the time all we really need is a meal, a bed or a toilet. It is not just the children: we also allow ourselves to become unhappy when all we need is one of those three basic requirements.

Within the family we need not only to discover what our needs are, but also to learn how to ask for what we need (Matt. 7.7–8). Often we are too proud to ask for something basic; then that unfulfilled need niggles and turns into a major sore point. If it does, the problem is our fault because we didn't take time to recognize the need and ask for it to be met. The person who asks receives (John 16.24; Jas. 4.2). We should be humble enough to let others know how they can help us. At the same time we need to be constantly aware of their needs and provide them even before they ask (Matt. 6.8).

CHAPTER XI
HOW MATINS ARE TO BE CARRIED OUT ON SUNDAYS

On Sundays the hour of rising for Matins should be earlier. In this Office the method is as follows. When the six Psalms and the versicle have been chanted, as we set out above, and all are seated in due order in their stalls, four readings should be read from the book (as we said before) with their responsories, and the **Glory be** *is chanted only in the fourth responsory. When he begins it all should rise at once with reverence. After these readings another six Psalms should follow in order with antiphons, as before, and a versicle. After these again four more lessons should be read with responsories, as set out before. Then three canticles from the prophets, as chosen by the Abbot, should be sung with Alleluia. When the verse has been said, the Abbot gives a blessing, and four more lessons are read from the New Testament in the way already described. After the fourth responsory the Abbot intones the hymn* **We praise you, O God**; *when this is finished the Abbot reads from the Gospel, while all stand in reverential honour. At the end of the reading all reply* **Amen**, *and then the Abbot begins the hymn* **To You Praise is due**, *and after the prayer, they begin Lauds. This order of Matins is to be kept on Sundays in both the summer and winter seasons — unless by chance they get up late (which should not happen) and some abridgement of the readings or responsories has to be made. But great care should be taken that this does not happen, but if it does, the person through whose*

*carelessness it has occurred must make adequate satisfaction to
God in the oratory.*

❦

In establishing longer services on Sunday, Benedict re-
affirms the first day of the week as the weekly celebration
of the resurrection. On Sundays there are extra 'alleluias',
the *Te Deum* is sung as well as an extra hymn of praise
after the gospel. Although Benedict doesn't require it,
there was a custom in his time for an all-night vigil to be
kept on Saturdays as a way of welcoming the weekly day
of resurrection. In chapter forty-eight he also lays down
the principle that there is to be no manual work on
Sundays. Instead there is to be more reading.

Benedict's specific liturgical rules do not seem to have
much to offer the modern Christian family; but once again
the rules point to underlying principles which are useful
to us. Benedict is clear that every Sunday is a holy day.
Since it is the Christian sabbath, we are obliged by the Ten
Commandments to keep it holy. There is increasing pressure from our society to abandon a traditional view of
Sunday. Shops and leisure facilities are open and we are
told that a 'Christian' Sunday is unsustainable in a multi-
cultural society. In fact Sunday is being spoiled simply to
feed the increasing greed of the shopkeeper who wants to
sell, the worker who wants to earn more and the consumer
who wants to buy more.

At the same time church leaders hesitate to lay down
strict Sabbatarian rules and regulations. So it is up to us to
work out how we can best obey God's commandments to
keep the Sabbath day holy. Benedict's rules can be
reduced to three principles: no work, more praise and
begin the night before.

So a good family Sunday begins on Saturday evening.
Every member of the family has a duty to be in church on
Sunday so together we need to consider what Saturday
night activities will help or hinder that commitment.
Sunday is a time of extra praise, but that doesn't simply
mean hymns and psalms. We should offer praise in the

larger sense by making Sunday a day of celebration. So we should plan a decent family meal, maybe inviting extra friends or family. We can also celebrate our family life together with special outings, creative projects and activities. In observing the Sabbath principle we should be reminded that 'the Sabbath was made for man, not man for the Sabbath' (Mark 2.27). Rules are there to help us live an abundant life, not a restricted life.

CHAPTER XII
HOW THE SOLEMN OFFICE OF LAUDS IS TO BE CARRIED OUT

Lauds on Sunday begin with Psalm 66, chanted continuously without an antiphon. After that, Psalm 50 is chanted with Alleluia. And then Psalm 117 and Psalm 62. Then the canticle **O All you Works of the Lord, Bless the Lord**, *and the* Praises, *a reading from the Apocalypse learnt by heart, a responsory, the hymn, the versicle, the canticle from the Gospels, and the litany to form the conclusion.*

☙

Here Benedict lays down the psalms and praises which the monks use to greet the dawn in the Office of Lauds. In an agrarian society with limited artificial light, the rising of the sun each day was an eloquent and beautiful reminder of the blessing of God which was fresh each morning. The monk, singing at sunrise, was singing God's praise with the whole of awakening creation. Taking time to see what psalms and praises Benedict requires will show us what a beautiful service of praise morning prayer can be.

As the sun rises the opening Psalm 66 (67) begins, 'Let God be gracious to us and bless us, let his face shine upon us'. Then the penitential Psalm 50 (51) is sung, followed by Psalm 117 (118), a psalm traditionally associated with the triumph of resurrection. The psalm in which we voice our thirsting for God, 62 (63), is followed by that ancient hymn from the book of Daniel in which the whole world praises the Creator. The praises are concluded with Psalms 148–150 which offer continual, universal praise to God. Even the memorized reading from Revelation was probably the paean of praise to the victorious Lamb of God from chapter 7.

These psalms and praises are all elementary words of worship for the Christian. As laymen we cannot maintain monastic offices of prayer, but we can use their treasury as part of our own prayers. If we get to know these psalms they will become a valuable resource for our own morning prayer. Most of them are laid down in the shorter forms of morning prayer available for our use. But if these formal prayers are too much we can use the psalms in more creative ways. We can memorize portions of these psalms and Scriptures and recite them when we get the chance each morning. If we drive to work we could have some of them on tape and recite them as we drive.

Within the family it is a good idea to take just a moment before the rush out of the house to school and work to offer the day to God. We can recite just one verse from these morning psalms antiphonally. So we could say, 'This is the day the Lord has made' to which the children reply, 'Let us rejoice and be glad in it!' (Ps. 118.24). When one verse is mastered we can move on to another one and so build up a repertoire of Scriptural praise and prayer which will lodge in our hearts and become a part of us.

CHAPTER XIII
How Lauds are Carried Out on Ordinary Days (a)

*On ordinary days the solemn Office of Lauds is to be carried out as follows: Psalm 66 is to be said without an antiphon, and rather slowly (as on Sunday) so that all may arrive in time for Psalm 50 which is to be chanted with an antiphon. After this, let two more Psalms be chanted, keeping to custom, namely: on Monday 5 and 35, on Tuesday 42 and 56, on Wednesday 63 and 64, on Thursday 87 and 89, on Friday 75 and 91, and on Saturday 142, and the canticle of Deuteronomy, divided into two parts. On each of the other days is sung a canticle from the prophets, as in the Roman Church. The **Praises** follow, and then a single reading from the Apostle to be recited by heart, the responsory, hymn, verse, canticle from the Gospels, and the litany to form the end.*

☙

The next few chapters of the Rule make dull reading. Benedict is simply taking the time to lay down the forms of the different monastic services. Again, the particular details of sixth-century monastic worship routine may not offer us high-flown spiritual counsel. These chapters will not inspire us with lofty sentiments and ecstatic spiritual experiences. They are not meant to.

In fact, a reading like today's takes us right down to the nitty-gritty and reminds us that for Benedict God is to be found in the details of life. Benedict could have written two books: one which dealt with 'spirituality', and one which dealt with practical matters. But he chose to put the two together in one Rule because the two must be woven together in the spiritual life. This is not just a matter of saying that our actions should match our words, and that we should try to live out the teachings which inspire us. It goes deeper than that. Benedictine spirituality is completely incarnational. As Jesus is God in particular human flesh at a particular historical time, so the particular details of our lives matter because that is where we find God hidden.

So today's dull reading reminds us to face the dull routine of daily life. Most days pass without great excitement or drama. What is our response to that? Are we always seeking the latest entertainment? Are we constantly running after a thrill, even if it is a spiritual thrill? Are we easily bored? Our modern consumer society encourages this constant, restless and immature seeking after entertainment, but Benedict brings us back to reality. God isn't found by chasing around. He is found by centring down, paying attention to detail and entering into the hidden blessedness of daily routine.

This doesn't mean the spiritual life is constant drudgery: only that the rewards are found in perseverance, not in seeking after thrills. The second vow of the Benedictine monk is to maintain stability of life. Stability means I must attend to the reality of this moment. Stability means I cannot seek escape. Stability means I must find God in this present moment because if I cannot find him here, I won't be able to find him anywhere.

CHAPTER XIII
HOW LAUDS ARE CARRIED OUT ON ORDINARY DAYS (B)

*Definitely neither Lauds nor Vespers should finish without the Lord's Prayer being recited at the end by the superior, while all listen. This is on account of the thorns of mutual offence which occur in the course of events; for in this way they are warned by the undertaking contained in the words of the prayer, **Forgive us as we forgive** and may cleanse their hearts from any defect of this kind. In the other Offices only the last part of this prayer is said, so that all may reply, **But deliver us from evil.***

Morning prayer (Lauds) and evening prayer (Vespers) should always finish with the Lord's Prayer. This simple expedient begins and ends the day with mutual forgiveness. This is extremely practical advice for any Christian family. Every day someone in the family will have a grumpy moment and snap out in anger or cruelty to another. It is so easy to let the little problems go unnoticed. It is especially easy to justify our loss of temper by our tiredness or the extreme circumstances. But overlooking the fault doesn't work. As Benedict points out, each little grievance is like a tiny thorn or splinter which gets under the skin. If it isn't picked out with the needle of forgiveness it can eventually poison the whole body.

This need for forgiveness is constant, and yet asking for forgiveness and granting forgiveness is the most difficult process in any relationship. It requires honesty and dangerous face-to-face confrontation. We go through all sorts of tricks and squirmings to avoid the face-off which honest forgiveness requires. So when we should ask forgiveness we bring our wives flowers or chocolates instead. When we should grant forgiveness we say, 'Oh, it didn't really matter'. When we should demand our children seek or grant forgiveness we overlook the grievance and brush it under the carpet.

Forgiveness becomes especially difficult if one person is willing to live a life of open-heartedness, but is met with a spouse or children who play defensive games. Sometimes the lack of openness is stubborn rebellion. More often it is lack of courage. Face-to-face forgiveness is tough because our defences have to come down, and we all hate being vulnerable. But when one person won't be open, the willing person in the relationship cannot forgive and be forgiven. Forgiveness has to be mutual: that's why Benedict enjoins his monks to say the Lord's Prayer corporately. The corporate prayer forces everyone to take part, but at the same time it allows those who are not courageous enough for face-to-face forgiveness to enter into the forgiveness gradually. Saying the Lord's Prayer together is a good tonic for family life too.

CHAPTER XIV
HOW MATINS ARE CARRIED OUT ON FEAST DAYS OF SAINTS

On the feasts of saints and on all solemn days Matins are to be carried out as we have laid down for Sundays, except that the Psalms, antiphons and readings proper to the day should be said; but the order of the Office should be as previously detailed.

Benedict doesn't say much about the saints in his Rule, but this short chapter shows that he was aware of the importance of the saints in the whole scheme of the spiritual life. In giving Saints' Days the same prominence as Sunday, he affirms that both the celebration of Sunday and the celebration of the Saints' Days are celebrations of the Paschal victory. In other words, the saints are honoured in a similar way to the resurrection because the victory of their lives shows the power of the resurrection at work. The perfection of humanity seen in the saints' lives is the perfection won for all of us through Christ's death and resurrection. So in the liturgy and life of the monastery the Saints' Days are celebrated with an equal joy.

According to Benedict the Christian life cannot be lived in independence. Even the hermits can only take up the solitary life after many years spent in community. Remembering the saints is another aspect of Benedict's emphasis on community. As we discover the lives of the saints we get to know members of our Christian family who have gone before us. Not only do they act as examples and guides, but our worship is joined with theirs around the throne of God (Rev. 7.9–end). So as we remember the Saints' Days our worshipping community is enlarged and our own perspective is taken up to the eternal dimension.

Perhaps in the past children were force-fed rather unrealistic stories of the saints. But there is no reason why biographies of the saints need to be either sentimental or falsely pious. The stories of both ancient and modern saints can be exciting and powerful examples for our children. There are some excellent resources to help make our families aware of the saints. Everything from animated films to storybooks and cassette tapes are available. Most children have plenty of entertaining secular videos. Why not get some which are entertaining *and* inspiring? Finally, it is a good idea for even very young children to learn about the saints, and to take some special ones as patrons. We might think it odd to have a friend in heaven. They won't.

CHAPTER XV
WHEN ALLELUIA IS TO BE SAID

From the holy feast of Easter until Pentecost Alleluia should be said throughout the Office both in the Psalms and in the responses.

From Pentecost till the beginning of Lent it should be said every night with the second group of Psalms only.

On every Sunday (outside Lent) the canticles of Matins, Lauds, Prime, Terce, Sext and None should be said with Alleluia; but Vespers should be sung with an antiphon.

Except from Easter to Pentecost, responsories are never to be said with Alleluia.

For Benedict the whole liturgical life turns on the hinge of our Lord's mighty resurrection. The use of 'Alleluia' is a sign of this emphasis. During Lent the alleluia is dropped completely as a sign of austerity, as a liturgical sign that we are going through the valley of temptation with Christ. Then on Easter day as Christ bursts from the tomb the great mysterious 'Alleluias' surge from the liturgy. The word 'alleluia' is Hebrew for 'Praise Jahweh'. It comes straight to us through Greek without being translated, and it is found in the Bible only in Revelation 19 where the multitudes in heaven give the victory shout of praise. So 'Alleluia' if you like, is the very language of heaven.

Benedict's words in this chapter seem dry, but beneath

them runs a fervour which ought to inspire us with pure joy and exhilaration. We are so timid and cynical, so shy of being triumphalist, and yet Christ has shattered the power of hell. He has defeated the powers of death forever. We are right to shout 'Alleluia!' with all the saints and angels because our God reigns supreme. This eternal Easter is at the very heart of Benedict's whole Rule. This is the victory we are running for, and this is the victory which gives us power to run on the path. So with the little word 'Alleluia' sprinkled throughout the liturgy between Easter and Pentecost, and then less so from Pentecost to the beginning of Lent, we are brought back time and time again to the power of Christ's victory alive and working through our lives with a dynamic force. Each Alleluia we utter, whether under our breath or at the top of our lungs, should be an intense and profound affirmation of the Easter victory at work in the world.

This element of praise should be a cornerstone of the Christian life. We should enable our families to see the Christ-life at work at all times blessing us, providing for us and bringing us together in love. Times of prayer should therefore include times of praise too; and as prayer needs practise to make perfect, so too we should practise praise – not just thanking God when we feel like it, but learning to thank him throughout the day. This will help us and our children very naturally to see his mighty hand in all his works.

CHAPTER XVI
HOW THE WORK OF GOD IS CARRIED OUT DURING THE DAYTIME

As the prophet puts it, 'Seven times daily I have praised you.' This sacred number of seven will be performed by us if we carry out the duties of our service at Lauds, Prime, Terce, Sext, None, Vespers and Compline, for it is of these hours of the day that he said, 'Seven times a day I have praised you.' And of the Night Office the same prophet said, 'At midnight I got up to give you praise.' Let us therefore at these times give praise to our Creator 'for his righteous judgements', that is to say at Lauds, Prime, Terce, Sext, None, Vespers and Compline, and at night let us get up to praise him.

In Benedict's time the monks went into church eight times a day for prayer and praise. But Benedict sees these eight services through the prism of Scripture, so he quotes Psalm 119.164: 'Seven times daily I have praised you', to indicate the seven daytime Offices, and Psalm 119.62: 'At midnight I got up to give you praise', to match up with the night Office. Maybe this method of interpretation is a little strained, and of course, very few monasteries maintain the full eight hours of prayer these days. Apart from anything else, the daily Mass has become a necessity, and modern hours of work and life do not permit a regime which was designed for the sixth century with its dependence on natural light and simple work.

If the monks cannot keep up such a regime, surely it is impossible for us to pray seven times a day. But in many ways we laymen have more opportunity to pray seven times a day. We can do so because we are not bound to the monastic Offices with their length and complexity. Furthermore, we have more control over our personal timetables. In fact, it may be very possible to construct seven small spaces for prayer within the normal day. Seven points of prayer might be: 1. On getting out of bed; 2. At breakfast; 3. At our mid-morning break; 4. At lunch; 5. At our mid-afternoon break; 6. At the evening meal; 7. At bedtime.

Of course these points of prayer can't be the recitation of numerous psalms, canticles, collects and antiphons. But they can be structured with the use of memorized prayers. Alternatively, they can simply be opportunities to take a few deep breaths, slow down the pace of life, say the Lord's Prayer and keep a few moments of meditative silence. This can be woven into our life and work in such a way that it soon becomes a healthy and life-giving habit.

If we punctuate our lives with prayer it will soon be natural for our children to do the same. Mealtimes are natural points of prayer in the daily routine. So are bedtimes and the moment before we go out of the door to work or school. Benedict liked seven prayer-times a day because seven was the mystical perfect number. Our job is to find the perfect, or natural, number of prayer points in our own routine, and then to build on them until prayer – and therefore the awareness of God – permeates our life and consciousness.

CHAPTER XVII

HOW MANY PSALMS ARE TO BE SAID AT THESE HOURS

*The order of the Psalmody at Matins and Lauds has already been dealt with; now we must consider the remaining hours. At Prime three Psalms should be said, separately, and not under one **Glory be**. The hymn is sung after the versicle, **O God come to my aid**, before beginning the Psalms. When the three Psalms are finished there should be one lesson, a versicle, **Lord have mercy** and the concluding prayers. The Offices of Terce, Sext and None are to be carried out in the same way, thus: the opening verse, the hymn of the hour, the three Psalms, a reading and verse, **Lord have mercy** and the concluding prayers. If the community is large enough antiphons should be used; otherwise the Psalms are sung straight through.*

For the evening prayer meeting four Psalms with antiphons will be enough. After them a lesson should be recited, then a responsory, a hymn, a versicle, a canticle from the Gospels, the litany and the Lord's Prayer at the end.

*For Compline the recitation of three Psalms, said straight through without an antiphon, is enough. After these there will be the hymn proper to this hour, a lesson, a versicle, **Lord have mercy**, and the blessing at the end.*

༚

Now Benedict begins two chapters laying down detailed structure for the monastic Offices. The two major prayer points in the day were the morning Office (Lauds) and the evening Office (Vespers). The other offices are sometimes called the 'Little Hours'. Outside the monastery we can only observe the 'Little Hours' inasmuch as we cultivate an awareness of God and attempt to punctuate our day with prayer at regular intervals.

Compline is the night Office of the monks. Consisting of the same three psalms every evening, plus a hymn, and a reading; it is a plea for God's protection through the dark hours of the night. These bedtime prayers of the monks can be a real point of peace and quiet for us too. Psalm 4 includes the beautiful verse, 'I will lay me down in peace and take my rest, for it is thou Lord only who makes me dwell in safety'. Psalm 91 invokes God's protection from evil through the night, while Psalm 134 closes the day in quiet praise. In our own stressful lives, Compline can be a still point at the end of the day when God can 'lift from our souls the strain and stress', and we can rest in his peace for a few moments before sleep. A good way to use Compline is to buy a disc of Gregorian chant with the Office of Compline on it: play it and follow along with the words each night until they become well-known. The music and words will move into a deep level of the mind and heart. Such an exercise deepens our prayer life, and has the practical benefit of helping us sleep well.

Psalm 134 is short and can be used at bedtime prayers with children. Bits of Psalm 91 are also good and the prayers of Compline make excellent bedtime prayers. An especially good one is found in the older Anglican form of Compline: *Be present O merciful God and protect us through the silent hours of this night, so that we who are wearied by the changes and chances of this fleeting world may repose upon thy eternal changelessness. AMEN.* This eloquent prayer has a fine cadence and is easy to memorize. When we use it with the children the whole family is linked with the great Benedictine tradition through the service of Compline.

CHAPTER XVIII
IN WHAT ORDER THE PSALMS SHOULD BE SAID (A)

*First should be said the verse, **O God come to my aid, Lord make haste to help me**, and **Glory be**; then the hymn of the hour.*

Then at Prime on Sunday are to be said four stanzas of Psalm 118; at the remaining hours, namely Terce, Sext and None, three stanzas of the same Psalm are to be said.

At Prime on Monday three Psalms, namely 1, 2 and 6 are to be said, and so on each day at Prime up to Psalm 19, continuing till Sunday (exclusively); but note that Psalms 9 and 17 are to be divided into two parts. In this way the Sunday Matins will always begin with Psalm 20.

This chapter is all nuts and bolts. There doesn't appear to be too much to glean from Benedict's necessary rota of which psalms for which Offices. But again, within the detail the heartbeat of the spiritual life can be discerned. In today's reading Benedict stipulates that each Office in the day should begin with the simple prayer, 'O God come to my assistance; O Lord make haste to help me' (Ps. 40.13). This prayer throbs like a heartbeat through the liturgical day. It is a simple plea which acknowledges our constant need for God's upholding power and grace.

Two hundred years before Benedict's time the first Christian monks went out into the deserts of Egypt, Palestine and

Arabia. Part of their quest was to discover the way to 'pray without ceasing' (1 Thess. 5.17). We know that by Benedict's time the monks at St Catherine's monastery on Mount Sinai were using a form of repetitive prayer, and that the 'Jesus Prayer' spread to the Greek monastic colony of Mount Athos and on into Russia and the West.

Thomas Merton tells us that the monastic tradition of *hesychia* or 'sweet repose' is a way of praying in which the monk repeats a word of Scripture over and over again until it becomes a part of his breathing, then part of his whole being, body and soul. One of these prayers is 'Lord Jesus Christ, Son of God, have mercy on me a sinner', but perhaps the older form is the 'word' Benedict uses here to begin the daily offices: 'O Lord come to my assistance; O Lord make haste to help me'.

This repetitive form of prayer suits some people and not others. It can provide a technique to deepen the prayer life and take us beyond words to the very depth of silence and peace. At best it helps us accomplish what Benedict aims for: a consciousness that is shifted from obsession with our own concerns to a constant awareness of God's presence and our deep need for his grace.

Within the family this phrase can function as a versicle and response before a prayer of thanks at table. So the person praying says, 'O Lord come to my assistance', to which everyone else responds, 'O Lord make haste to help me'. Little things like this help make connections and weave tradition into our daily life in an easy and practical way.

CHAPTER XVIII

IN WHAT ORDER THE PSALMS SHOULD BE SAID (B)

At Terce, Sext and None on Mondays are to be said the nine remaining stanzas of Psalm 118, three at each hour. Psalm 118 is thus finished on two days, Sunday and Monday; on Tuesday three Psalms are to be chanted at each of Terce, Sext and None, from 119 to 127, nine Psalms in all. And these Psalms are to be repeated daily at the same hours until Sunday; but the arrangement of hymns, readings and verses is to follow the same pattern daily, and on Sunday a new beginning should be made with Psalm 118.

༄

The monks are to recite the entire psalter in one week. To do this they have to get through all one hundred and seventy-six verses of Psalm 119 at different Offices on Sunday and Monday. So this longest of the psalms is accomplished in two days. Psalm 119 is not only the longest, but it is unique in its content, for the whole psalm is a meditation on the word of God. Nearly every verse in the psalm refers to the word of God, either as God's precepts, his commandments, his promises, his decrees or his testimonies. In virtually every verse the psalmist brings us back to the word of God in praise.

Perhaps Benedict placed this psalm at the beginning of the week so that it would act as a foundation for the rest of the week's praises. Like a constant heartbeat, the monks would praise God for the goodness of his eternal Word. The pre-eminence of this psalm shows us how Benedict used Scripture, and teaches us some valuable truths about the use of Scripture in our own lives.

Benedict's Rule is imbued with Scripture. He rarely uses Scripture to provide proof texts for his beliefs. Instead the Scripture is woven into the very fabric of the Rule. As it is woven into the Rule, so it was woven into Benedict's life. Psalm 119.11 says 'I have hidden your word in my heart, that I might not sin against you'. So Benedict and his monks would have memorized huge portions of the psalms, burying the words in their hearts so that they might blossom in their lives.

This is the monastic attitude to the Scriptures. They are to be studied and understood with the mind, but more importantly, they are to be hidden in the heart. They are to be kept as fuel for meditation. We are told elsewhere that the 'Word of God is living and active, sharper than a two-edged sword, able to divide soul and spirit and judge the thoughts and intentions of the heart' (Heb. 4.12). So through regular reading, discussion and education our whole family should become more knowledgeable about the Scriptures; then as we learn how to understand and apply the Word of God it will be woven into our own lives, as it was for Benedict.

CHAPTER XVIII
IN WHAT ORDER THE PSALMS SHOULD BE SAID (C)

Vespers are to be sung each day with four Psalms, beginning with Psalm 109 and ending with Psalm 147, but excluding those which are assigned to other hours, namely Psalms 117–27, 133 and 142; the rest are all to be said at Vespers. Since, however, there are three Psalms too few, the longer Psalms of those just mentioned, namely 138, 143, 144 are to be divided into two. On the other hand Psalm 116, being very short, is to be joined with 115.

This covers the order of the Psalms for Vespers: all the other items, namely the reading, responsory, hymn, versicle and canticle, are to be performed as we have laid down above. At Compline the same Psalms are to be repeated daily, namely 4, 90 and 133.

⁊

Having dealt with 'Little Hours' Benedict goes on to give instructions for saying Vespers. Vespers, or evening prayer, is the second hinge of the monastic day of prayer. These two major Offices are the most important ones, and they are the ones we should try to follow if we can.

In a busy family the point when Vespers should be said is the most chaotic. Between 4 and 7 p.m. everyone is tired, hungry and irritable. But a meal needs to be made, homework needs to be done. At the same time there is pressure for us to spend 'quality time' together every day. How can any busy family fit evening prayer into the whole routine?

Someone has well said that when he makes time for prayer he always seems to have time for everything else. When he doesn't make time for prayer there is never enough time for anything else. This is a question of priorities. When we put first things first, everything else falls into place. So it is necessary to make time for family prayers together in the evening. A slightly longer grace at the evening meal is one way to weave evening prayer into family life. Alternatively, some families have a prayer both before *and* after the evening meal. Others make room for family prayers just before bed. However it happens, the evening prayer-time should be structured and a flexible routine should be established.

There are some excellent resources for family prayers. Books of prayers for children, illustrated Bible story books and illustrated lives of saints are but a few. Children love ritual. They love having a special place for prayer, so light some candles and have evening prayers in the same place most nights. It is useful too, to have a simple structure. Start by making the sign of the cross and saying together, 'In the name of the Father, the Son and the Holy Spirit'. Then a Bible story, maybe a short section of the psalms in the form of a chorus or chant, and then informal prayers which ask God for specific needs as well as offering praise and thanks. The Lord's Prayer, 'Glory Be' or 'Hail Mary' is a good way to finish. After the prayers silence should be kept, even if only for thirty seconds or so.

CHAPTER XVIII
IN WHAT ORDER THE PSALMS SHOULD BE SAID (D)

This settles the order of the Psalms during the day: all the remaining Psalms are to be divided equally into the seven vigils of the night: twelve are to be allotted to each night, but dividing the Psalms of greater length.

Nevertheless, we emphasise that if anyone is dissatisfied with this arrangement of the Psalms, he is to organise them otherwise as he finds better; he should, however, see to it that the Psalter be recited every week, starting anew from vigils of the Lord's Day. For monks who in the course of a week sing less than the Psalter with its usual canticles manifest a service too slothful for their dedicated state, since we read that our holy Fathers vigorously completed in a single day what it is to be hoped we who are tepid may accomplish in a whole week.

⁂

There are two final points to observe in this chapter. Firstly, Benedict sets out the psalms without too much attention to some master plan which would place them thematically within the week's worship. Neither does he come up with a great scheme which assigns certain psalms for the different parts of the church year. Such a 'clever' scheme would very quickly become predictable and unbearably routine.

Instead, for the most part, the psalms are to be said consecutively. In Benedict's more 'random' scheme each psalm simply stands on its own merits as it comes up each week. Without a pre-set liturgical agenda it will be both familiar and fresh. But within the eucharistic lectionary we are given the Scripture in a thematic and liturgical framework. We do well to read Scripture within that framework, but we should also sit down and read a gospel or an epistle straight through, thus getting an overall understanding and a freshness which we cannot get when the Scripture is read liturgically. Likewise, reading a children's Bible story book from Genesis through to Revelation helps them see the whole thread of salvation history in the Bible.

Finally, this chapter shows Benedict's essentially humble nature once again. He has troubled himself to set out an order for the recitation of the psalter, but he is quite happy for others to come up with a better scheme. While the psalms are an essential cornerstone of monastic worship, the particular order is not essential. In family life we need a very flexible approach to worship and prayer. The needs of each individual must be taken into consideration. So must the changing needs of the family as the children grow older and circumstances change. Prayer is essential: the particular routine is not.

As usual Benedict is strict as well as tolerant. Others may change the order of the psalms, but they are still to recite the entire psalter in one week, otherwise they are slacking. We may have to be flexible in the ordering of our family prayers and worship, but we also have to be firm. It is easy to become too slack ourselves, and then not bother to train our children in the duty and joy of prayer. Benedict goads his monks on by reminding them of those holy fathers in the desert who recited the psalter once every day. In a similar way we should be goaded on by the greater examples of the monks whose lives and work we are seeking to reflect.

CHAPTER XIX
RECOLLECTION IN CHANTING

We believe that God is present everywhere, and that the eyes of the Lord are in every place, keeping watch on the good and the bad; but most of all should we believe this without any shadow of doubt, when we are engaged in the work of God. We should therefore always be mindful of the prophet's words, 'Serve the Lord with fear.' And again, 'Sing wisely.' And yet again, 'In the sight of the angels I will sing to you.' We must therefore consider how we should behave in the sight of the Divine Majesty and his Angels, and as we sing our Psalms let us see to it that our mind is in harmony with our voice.

❧

Catherine Wybourne has translated the title of this chapter: 'On the Discipline of Singing the Psalms'. It sums up Benedict's point a bit better. Here at the end of his section on the structure of the liturgy Benedict comes to the heart of the matter. Echoing the Prologue, we are to be awake to the fact that God is always present keeping watch (Prov. 15.3). We should be aware of this fact especially when praying, and so should pray with godly fear (Ps. 2.11) and respect.

This constant awareness of God should keep our mind in harmony with our voice. But harmony between the inner and outer lives isn't easy. We often think the solution to hypocrisy is to change our outward behaviour so that our words and deeds conform to what we believe, in other words, to practise what we preach. Change on the outside is one thing, but the struggle to change on the inside is even more demanding, and outer goodness without an inner transformation is the worst hypocrisy.

Benedict teaches that meditation on the word of God is a way for that inner change to take place. Harmony between mind and words means harmony between our mind and God's word. So St Paul calls us not to be conformed to the world, but to be transformed by the renewing of our minds (Rom. 12.2). This doesn't just mean we should concentrate more during prayer. Instead, Benedict wants our prayer to be a dynamic force which transforms us completely.

This little phrase – that our minds should be in harmony with our words – takes us to the heart of the Benedictine vow to pursue *conversatio morum*, conversion of life. Esther de Waal points out that the vow to conversion of life is a 'commitment to total inner transformation'. This total conversion is no less than dying to ourselves and living as new men in Christ Jesus (Rom. 6.11). Always aware of God's presence with us, we strive to live with our minds in harmony with the Word of God (Eph. 4.22–24). This is not just a theory. The risen Christ really is at work with us to effect this transformation. Commitment to this *conversatio morum* or complete transformation is the best service we can offer our families too, because the more we are transformed into his likeness the more they will have Christ as their father and husband.

CHAPTER XX
REVERENCE AT PRAYER

If we wish to bring anything to the attention of powerful men, it is only with humility and reverence that we dare to do so. How much more then should we present our supplications to the Lord God of all things with complete humility and devout purity of mind. Indeed we must grasp that it is not by using many words that we shall get our prayers answered, but by purity of heart and repentance with tears. Prayer, therefore, should be short and pure, unless on occasion it be drawn out by the feeling of the inspiration of divine grace. In community, however, the prayer should be kept quite short, and when the superior gives the sign all should rise together.

⟡

This concise teaching on prayer ends the section on how prayer should be ordered. But it also comes at the middle of the Rule. Rightly so, for it lies at the very heart of Benedict's whole teaching on the spiritual life. The little phrase, we should pray with 'purity of mind', is the key. Dom Cary-Elwes points out that this phrase 'purity of heart' or 'purity of mind' is translated from the Greek *apatheia*. In Greek philosophy this word meant 'detachment' or a cold, Stoic insensibility. A similar concept still exists in some popular forms of Eastern spirituality.

But the Desert Fathers some hundred years or so before Benedict had the wisdom to translate the term as 'pure devotion' or 'purity of heart'. So Christian contemplative prayer is not detached from the world. Instead, as Cary-

Elwes says, it is 'a deep longing or attachment with all our heart, mind, soul and strength and all our being for God'. Subsequently the Christian is also attached to all other created things with a love which flows from his primary attachment and longing for the Creator himself. The pure Christian heart is 'detached' from created things not because he despises them, but because he loves their Creator more.

This pure condition of mind and heart is the goal of the monks' vow of *conversatio morum* or conversion of life. All the psalms, all the prayer, all the obedience and silence, are bent to this one end. Benedict links such pure and radiant devotion for God with humility and recognizes that by these two inner qualities, and not through many words, our prayers are honoured. As a result, our prayers should be short and pure. God loves the prayer which the author of the *Cloud of Unknowing* calls 'a dart of longing love'. These arrow prayers are the natural cries for help and the spontaneous words of thanks and praise which we offer up to God. We should practise this form of prayer and encourage our children to speak with God naturally and spontaneously.

Benedict also says that communal prayer should be short. As Jesus himself points out, there is no virtue in long public prayers. In fact, we ought to be suspicious of the person who makes long prayers (Mark 12.38–40). Lengthy prayers are not only a dreadful way of showing off, but they weary others, and make them resentful. So our family prayers should be brief, personal and to the point.

CHAPTER XXI
OF DEANS OF THE MONASTERY

If the community is rather large, brethren of good reputation and holy way of life should be selected from among them and appointed deans. They are to exercise care over their deaneries in all respect according to the commandments of God and the instructions of their Abbot. They should be chosen as deans who are such that the Abbot may be able to share his burdens with them with confidence. They should not be chosen according to seniority but for their merits and their wisdom in teaching. And if any of these deans, becoming inflated with some form of pride, be found worthy of rebuke, he is to be corrected once, twice, indeed three times; but if he will not amend, he should be removed and another who is worthy should be substituted for him. And we lay down the same procedure for the Prior of the Monastery.

❧

Having dealt with prayer, Benedict now begins a section on administration and discipline in the monastery. The dean was appointed as an overseer of ten monks. Benedict had personal experience of rebellion in the ranks. Once when he was an abbot his monks tried to poison him, and he left them in disgust. But this experience didn't make him cling to power in a tyrannical way. Instead, he sees the absolute need for the abbot to have co-workers to share the burden of leadership in confidence. They are not

to be chosen according to their social rank or their seniority in the monastery, but according to their merits and
wisdom.

If we are in a position of leadership at work, in the
parish or at home, it is sometimes difficult to choose
people for promotion simply on merit. Seniority, a better
education or a better social standing always seem like
attractive qualities. But it is exactly these qualities which
often end up making the second echelon of leaders proud.
In the absence of real leadership skills they rely on their
seniority, social rank or educational achievements to
command respect. Better to search out the humble person
whose gifts are hidden.

Once again, Benedict's understanding of human nature
is profound. Appointing a dean for his innate skills rather
than his outward status is another aspect of Benedict's
principle that the gifts and personality of each member of
the monastery should be recognized and nurtured. The
same principle is vital in the home. Each child will have
certain gifts and certain faults. It is up to us to discover
and develop the gifts while we also work with them to
overcome the weaknesses.

Benedict's advice that the abbot share the burden with
confidence in the dean is a good pattern for our marriage
relationship. We must bear one another's burdens, both in
our relationship with each other, and in our relationship
with the children. Bearing one another's burdens (Gal. 6.2)
requires constant open communication, yet so often we
suffer in silence and soldier on until the burden becomes
too great and there is an emotional explosion. The last part
of today's chapter tells us what causes this sullen breakdown in the relationship. Pride keeps us from taking other
people's burdens and from sharing our own with them.
Sharing our burdens is a sign of humility, and humility is
the foundation of life in the Spirit.

February 27 (or 28)
June 29
October 29

CHAPTER XXII
HOW THE MONKS SHOULD SLEEP

The brethren are to sleep each in a single bed. These beds are assigned to them in order according to the length of their monastic life, subject to the Abbot's discretion. If it is possible, all should sleep in one place, but if their numbers do not permit this, they should take their rest by tens or twenties with the seniors who are entrusted with their care. A candle should burn continuously in this room till morning. They should sleep clothed, girt with girdles or cords, but not with their knives at their sides as they sleep, for fear that a brother should be wounded while asleep. And so let the monks be always ready, and when the signal is given, they should get up without delay and make haste to arrive first for the Work of God, but in a gentle and orderly way. The younger brethren should not have their beds together, but dispersed among the seniors. When they get up for the Work of God they may quietly encourage one another since the sleepy are given to making excuses.

In this intimate chapter we get to peek into the monk's dormitory fifteen hundred years ago. In the year 535 the Emperor Justinian decreed that monks should sleep in dormitories to avoid sexual immorality, and Benedict probably has some similar safeguards in mind with the guidelines he lays down here. But it would be wrong to see this chapter only in those terms. Most of the rules for the dormitory are aids for getting out of bed for the midnight Office of Vigils. That this is his main aim is seen in the tender instruction of the last verse: 'When they get up ... they may quietly encourage one another since the sleepy are given to making excuses'.

But Esther de Waal points out a deeper significance to this chapter. As we have seen in the chapters on the Office of Vigils, rising in the night was spiritually meaningful, for the monk is meant to 'awake out of sleep' and engage in 'spiritual warfare' in the night. Furthermore, there are living echoes here of Jesus' parable in Matthew 25 about the wise and foolish virgins. A candle burns in the dormitory as the lamps had to be kept lit while the virgins watched for the bridegroom. Although the monks sleep they do so in their clothes, ready to spring out of bed to 'meet the bridegroom' in the Office of Vigils. In the story the virgins even wake one another up and encourage one another as Benedict tells his monks to do. And the story ends with the watchword of the Benedictine life: 'Therefore keep watch because you do not know the day or the hour'.

So the most mundane things of life are imbued with meaning for Benedict. The sleeping arrangements become a living parable and a constant reminder of the need for the monk to be spiritually alert and aware of God's presence. The same thing can be applied in our homes. If we see with sacramental eyes, all the details of life can become pointers to a deeper reality. So the night-light in the hall can signify the watchful spirit. Our routine of prayer at bedtime and rising should be simple and natural, but also deeply significant. If we cultivate this way of seeing, our ordinary lives can surge with meaning. If we share it with our children they will develop a curiosity and fascination with the meaning within all things.

CHAPTER XXIII
EXCOMMUNICATION FOR FAULTS

If any brother is found to be contumacious or disobedient or arrogant or a grumbler or one who sets himself up against some point of the Holy Rule or despises the ordinances of his seniors, he is to be warned privately once or twice, according to our Lord's command, by his superiors. If he does not amend his ways, then he should be publicly rebuked before all. If he still does not improve let him undergo excommunication, if he understands the nature of this punishment. If, however, he is stubborn, he must undergo corporal punishment.

⟞

In the next few chapters Benedict specifies types and forms of discipline for the monastery. The rules are appropriate for the sixth century, and we are tempted to gloss over them as outmoded and crude. But why should Benedict's attitude be inferior or less understanding and sympathetic simply because it is fifteen hundred years old? We might blame Benedict for violence, but our society is far more violent than his was. In fact, Benedict's disciplinary rules prove to be compassionate and gentle, and the principles he lays down are invaluable for the ordering of our family life.

In today's chapter Benedict points out the major faults of the monk. They are stubbornness, disobedience, pride and grumbling. Every family struggles with these human faults daily. Grumbling is especially nasty because the grumbler nurtures his selfish pride in a sullen way. As Benedict says in chapter two, these faults are to be rooted out like noxious weeds. They must be dealt with early because they lead to the worst of human sins. Furthermore, these basic faults are a sin against community because they undermine authority and spread discontent like a cancer.

But if Benedict is adamant that stubbornness, grumbling and disobedience are rooted out, he is also careful to establish a just and gentle code of discipline. Following the gospel example in Matthew 18.15–16, the superiors are to warn the offender once or twice privately. Then he should be rebuked publicly. Excommunication follows and corporal punishment is kept as a last resort. This is a simple and effective way to maintain discipline in the home. Too often we try to be nice and avoid all conflict and unpleasant discipline. But it is impossible to keep this up, and eventually we snap and lash out in uncontrolled violence – either verbal or physical.

Instead we should use warnings first, isolation second and only resort to a controlled and tempered form of corporal punishment if all else fails. This is not only helps us keep control, but the child also knows exactly where he or she stands. A sentimental avoidance of strict discipline does no one good. When we finally lash out in rage the child sees our unpredictability and learns fear. They also learn that uncontrolled rage is acceptable and soon respond in the same way by screaming and hitting others uncontrollably.

CHAPTER XXIV

HOW EXCOMMUNICATION IS
TO BE REGULATED

Excommunication or disciplinary measures should be propor-
tionate to the nature of the fault, and the nature of faults is for
the Abbot to judge. If then a brother is found to commit less
serious faults he is to be deprived of sharing in the common
meal. The rules for one who is thus excluded from the sharing in
the common meal will be: he may not intone antiphon or Psalm
in the oratory; nor may he read a lesson until he has made satis-
faction. He must eat alone after the meal of the brethren. Thus if
they eat at the sixth hour, he will eat in the evening; until
having made adequate satisfaction he receives pardon.

෨

When Benedict speaks of excommunication he means
isolation from the community, not denial of eucharistic
communion. The disciplinary principles he sets down here
are wise and restrained. They are designed to educate and
reform the monks, remembering that the words 'discipline' and 'disciple' both come from the Latin word 'to
teach' (Prov. 12.1).

The first disciplinary principle Benedict lays down is
that the sanction should be proportionate to the nature of
the fault. This has two elements: first, that the severity of
the sanction should match the seriousness of the fault.
Secondly, that the sort of punishment should match the
wrongdoing. So Benedict uses isolation from the commu-

nity because the stubborn, grumbling and disobedient monk has, by his actions and attitude, shown himself to be unfit company. The extent of the isolation matches the seriousness of his fault. This is fair and logical.

Isolation is also a fair punishment to use in the home. If a child's behaviour is obnoxious he should be separated so that everyone else will be spared his bad behaviour. Children can be sent to their room; in some homes a special chair in a room is reserved for isolation. Isolation is effective if the amount of isolation suits the child's misdemeanour. The manner of isolating the child is important. He or she should never be isolated with sarcasm or personal comments which make the isolation a personal rejection. Instead it must be emphasized that they are being separated because their behaviour is troubling the rest of the family.

Isolation needn't be terrible. Appropriate isolation can also be combined with a creative correction which matches the crime. So a child who screams disrespectfully could be asked to keep silence for a time. One who will not clean their room can be asked to go somewhere on their own and write a story about what would happen if everyone were untidy all the time. A child with bad table manners could be put at their own table for a meal until they learn to behave better.

In all these things, it is vital that isolation is designed not to reject but to correct the child. Isolation also carries a deeper message. At the foundation level, selfishness separates us from God and from other people. Once separated, we better understand the need for reconciliation and return. Isolation teaches a spiritual lesson too. It gently reminds us that the ultimate separation is hell itself, while heaven is the eternal communion of God's whole family.

March 2
July 2
November 1

CHAPTER XXV
VERY SERIOUS FAULTS

The brother who is guilty of a very serious fault is to be suspended from sharing in the meals and also from the oratory. None of the brethren may associate with him in companionship or conversation. He is to be left alone at the work assigned to him and to remain in penitent grief as he reflects on the terrible sentence of the Apostle. 'This kind of man is handed over to bodily death, so that his spirit may be saved for the day of the Lord.' His food he should take alone in such measure and at such time as the Abbot thinks most suitable for him; nor may he or the food that is given him receive a blessing from anyone who passes by.

Now Benedict deals with the more serious offences. The isolation of the brother becomes more severe: he cannot share in common meals; he is excluded from common worship and common work. His food is taken alone, and he gets only the food which the abbot thinks he deserves. As Benedict mentions fasting as a punishment in chapter thirty, this means the offending monk's solitary meals are probably pretty meagre.

It is true that Benedict allows for corporal punishment, but here we see that he uses a whole range of appropriate punishments instead of beatings. As the wrongdoing becomes more serious, the isolation is increased, and other more unpleasant punishments are added. Isolation is still the main sanction in order forcibly to illustrate that being a member of a family or community requires decent behaviour. Isolation also gives the offender time to think about his fault and take responsibility for his own improvement. Even so, Benedict points out that this more severe isolation is only for the brother who 'is guilty of a very serious fault'.

As the children get older, isolation is still the best form of discipline. The principle of isolation can be applied in many different ways which are appropriate to the problem. As Benedict uses additional fasts as a punishment, so treats shouldn't go to those who are badly behaved. An older child can be isolated from some activity they enjoy such as television or outings with friends, and even teenagers will still feel it a punishment if they are made to sit still in isolation for a time. Once again, this isolation can also be used as a creative time. Instead of simply taking away television or depriving the child of an outing, the time alone can be used to help them reflect on why they are being punished. They can use the time to practise an instrument, do some housework or write a story about why they're being corrected.

Once isolation is understood as the primary means of discipline in a family there is nothing wrong with asking the disobedient child what he or she regards as a fair punishment. This decision-making involves them in the process of discipline, and helps them see the parental point of view. Quite often they will choose a punishment far more severe than they deserve. The ultimate decision is still the parents', but to consult with the child gives them dignity and helps them take responsibility for their own actions and attitudes.

CHAPTER XXVI
UNAUTHORISED ASSOCIATION WITH THE EXCOMMUNICATED

If any brother, acting without instructions from the Abbot, takes it upon himself to associate with an excommunicated brother in any way, or to talk with him, or send him a message, he must likewise undergo the punishment of excommunication.

Benedict is firm that the punishment of a troublemaker is not simply the concern of the abbot. The whole community works together to uphold the discipline which the abbot puts in place. Should a monk communicate with his isolated brother, that monk must share his punishment and be isolated as well. This is not an arbitrary rule, for in breaking the code of the community the monk deserves to be outside it for a time.

While this rule seems hard on first reading, it is easy to see why it is necessary. For a community to live together in peace the authority structure must be maintained by all. Benedict had experience of a mutinous band of monks, and understood all too well how easy it is for people to take sides; for factions to develop and rebellion to foment.

A gritty kind of love is necessary on this one because when someone in the family is being punished emotions run high. Disciplining children is a high-risk enterprise, and it is one of the areas where husband and wife most often fall out, one spouse often pleading for clemency while the other is intent on being strict. But parents must be united in their discipline of the children. If not, the children will soon learn to play one parent against another. Before long favourites are chosen, factions develop, resentment builds and the whole family is at war. Likewise, children must not take sides against their parents. If the discipline enacted is fair and logical then everyone must agree to support the regime, knowing that when it is their turn to be disciplined they will want equally fair treatment.

If the whole family is to support a fair and logical regime of discipline then all the more reason to make sure the system is set up and agreed on first by the parents, and then by the whole family. When children and parents agree on a system of rewards and sanctions which they will honour together, the actual sanctions themselves are almost never needed.

While taking sides with one being punished is not permitted, we will see in the next chapter that Benedict does allow sympathy and support for the punished brother. Likewise in the family, while no one must take sides with the person being disciplined, the other parent and the siblings can rightly offer sympathy and support. It is possible to offer sympathy without taking sides. Such unconditional sympathy is more likely to bring the wrongdoer back to make his peace with confidence and real repentance.

CHAPTER XXVII
THE CONCERN THE ABBOT MUST HAVE FOR THE EXCOMMUNICATED

*The Abbot should carry out with the deepest concern his respon-
sibility for the brethren who fall into sin, 'for it is not those who
are in good health who need a doctor, but those who are sick.' For
this reason he should, like a skilful doctor, use every possible
remedy; for example he may send* senpectae *(that is, mature
and wise brethren) to give unofficial consolation to their waver-
ing brother, and induce him to make humble satisfaction, and
give him comfort, 'so that he is not overcome by too much
sadness.' And so let it be as the Apostle also says, 'that love is
reaffirmed towards him'; and everybody is to pray for him.*

*It is indeed very important that the Abbot should show his
concern, and make speed to employ his skill and energy, lest he
lose one of the sheep entrusted to him. For he must bear in mind
that it is the care of sick souls that he has undertaken, not a
despotic rule over healthy ones. Moreover, he should fear the
threats of the prophet, through whose words God says, 'What
you saw to be fat you took, and what was weak you threw away.'
And let him copy the loving example of the Good Shepherd who
left the ninety-nine sheep on the mountains, and went away to
search for the one that had gone astray; and had such pity for its
weakness that he deigned to lay it on his own sacred shoulders,
and so carry it back to the flock.*

Right in the middle of these chapters which are sometimes called 'the penal code', we have one of the most tender and loving passages of the whole Rule. Here Benedict shows us the character of the true *abba*. It must be a self-portrait as well, for as Benedict's biographer, Pope Gregory the Great, said: 'He could not have written what he did not live himself'.

With his comparison of the abbot to a physician, Benedict makes clear that the driving reason for all the discipline is not simply order and peace in the community, but the healing of the sin-wounded soul (Matt. 9.12). So the true *abba* is a compassionate healer. He is also like the good shepherd who goes to any length to seek and to save the lost sheep (Luke 15.4–5). When we are struggling to maintain discipline in the family it is easy to lose sight of our real vocation. We get caught up in the minutiae, and only hope for the good behaviour and respect which allows us a peaceful life. But, of course, our real purpose for discipline in the home is a spiritual one. Like the abbot, we are concerned about the formation and development of the souls put in our charge. So each occasion of discipline has a higher goal.

This chapter also reminds us that love is at the heart of discipline (Prov. 3.12). Parents who read all the right child-care books and bring up their children according to all the best advice, but are not overflowing with love, will produce spoiled textbook children. In the same way parents who provide all the goods things money can buy, but don't give themselves to their children, will be failures. But the parents whose hearts are filled with unconditional love for their children can make many mistakes and still succeed. They can be financially poor and physically exhausted. They might limp from one crisis to another as seeming failures, but if there is deep, abiding and unconditional love the home will be filled with joy and they will be successful parents. So all the discipline in our homes must be fired by love, not just our human love, but the love which comes from God. If we live in that kind of love then we also live in God and God lives in us (1 John 4.16).

CHAPTER XXVIII

THE INCORRIGIBLE

If any brother who has been often corrected for some fault, and even been excommunicated, does not amend his way, he must receive harsher punishment, that is to say, he must suffer a beating. But if, even after this, he does not amend or if – which God forbid – he is so filled with pride as to want to defend his actions, then the Abbot must act like a wise doctor. If he has made use of poultices, of the ointments of his counsels, of the remedies of Divine Scripture, if he has come at last to the cautery of excommunication, and the blows of the rod, and if he now sees that his work is unavailing – let him make use of what is still greater: his own prayer combined with that of all the brethren that the Lord to whom nothing is impossible may work the salvation of the sick brother.

But if even by this means he is not cured then the Abbot must employ the surgeon's knife, as the Apostle says, 'Drive out the wicked man from among you.' And again, 'If the unfaithful one leaves you, let him go,' for fear that one diseased sheep may infect the whole flock.

☙

Benedict has likened the abbot to a physician, and he extends the analogy when he considers how the persistent offender is to be treated. The poultice of private admonition was meant to draw out the infection. The ointment of gentle counsel was designed to soothe and heal. The medicine of Scripture was meant to penetrate to the innermost part of the soul (Heb. 4.12). Isolation and corporal punishment were meant to cauterize the running wound with a painful but effective treatment. But if the illness of stubbornness, rebellion and hard-heartedness continues the only thing left is the surgeon's knife. The offender must be expelled from the monastery.

But in all this, Benedict calls one last time for prayer to be used as a cure. The abbot and all the brethren are to pray for the sin-sick brother. Just as we pray ardently for the cure of a person suffering from cancer, so Benedict calls for us to pray for the recovery of a brother or sister sick with a rebellious nature.

Benedict's hard, but realistic advice is necessary for the home as well. Sometimes, despite our best efforts, a child will turn out to be a bad one. For some inexplicable reason, a person chooses evil and not good. What is to be done with a child who refuses to be trained, refuses to fit in and despises everything good whenever he gets the chance? We are all prepared for teenaged rebellion, but what if that rebellion is aggressive, pervasive and completely incorrigible? What happens when we have prayerfully and carefully been gentle, then progressively more firm, and still nothing works? When worse comes to worst the child must leave the home. If every entreaty is spurned, if they have set their face on a course of destruction and their rebellion is actually harming the other siblings, then, provided they are old enough, they must go.

If all else fails in a relationship, then separation is the only choice. However, separation does not mean disowning the child. And in marriage a separation does not mean divorce. Although expulsion from the community of the family takes place, the door must always be left open. The father of the prodigal son is our example here. The son left, but the father was forever longing for his return.

CHAPTER XXIX
WHETHER BRETHREN WHO LEAVE SHOULD BE TAKEN BACK

If a brother has through his own wrong choice left the monastery and wants to come back again, he must first promise to make amendment for having left, and then let him be taken back in the lowest place as a test of his humility. If he goes away a second time, he may be received back, and even a third time; but after that he must realise that the path of return will not be granted him again.

✎

Expulsion from the monastery or from the family is a terrible and drastic final solution. Everything must be done to avoid such a rift. But if a monk does leave, Benedict allows them to return not just once, but three times. But if they choose to return, the seriousness of the problem is recognized by a penance. They must take the lowest place in the community.

Underlying this chapter is the figure of the father in the story of the prodigal son. He is the one who stands at the gate constantly looking for any sign of the estranged son. When the son is finally reconciled the father calls for the celebration to begin.

The same thing applies to our family life. If something terrible happens and a child or a spouse leaves the home, they must be readmitted at once with instant forgiveness. Benedict only allows three homecomings. In the Christian family a person's crime must be very serious indeed for the door ever to be closed for good. The poet Robert Frost has written, 'Home is the place where, when you have to go there, they have to take you in'. In virtually every other aspect of life our value is based on our achievement, but in the home love should never be, and never appear to be, conditional. We may approve of good behaviour and disapprove of poor performance, but that approval and disapproval must never be linked with our love for the child. From the earliest moment they must know our love covers both their good and their bad behaviour.

So the family is the one place where each person should be able to find constant, unfailing and unconditional love. No matter what the disagreement, separation or sin, our children must know that the door is always open. This requires a huge sacrifice on our part, for we must agree to be vulnerable. We must lay down the human instinct to bear a grudge. In allowing a difficult spouse or child to return we lay ourselves open to more rejection, stress and trouble. But if we are to mirror Christ as Christian fathers, then this is our role. In offering this kind of love to our children we reflect God's unconditional love for us, and our homes become a glimpse of heaven itself: that home which will one day welcome our rebel souls.

CHAPTER XXX
HOW BOYS ARE TO BE CORRECTED

Disciplinary measures should be appropriate to every age and intelligence: hence when boys or youths or others, incapable of understanding how serious a punishment excommunication is, commit offences, such persons are to suffer additional fasts or painful stripes, so that they may be cured.

❧

At various places in the Rule Benedict allows for corporal punishment. Of course he is not condoning abuse of any kind, and here he makes it clear when and why corporal punishment is appropriate. In his day there would have been boys in the monastery, and if they do not take the punishment of isolation seriously, then they must be disciplined with more physical means – a reduction in rations or sharp strokes.

It is 'politically correct' to shy away from corporal punishment, but restrained physical punishment should be compared to the alternatives. Is it better for the child or a parent simply to give in to their bad behaviour? Is it better for the adult to lose his temper and scream abuse at a child? Emotional damage is far easier to inflict and far harder to erase than a short, but necessary smack. Benedict realizes that physical punishment of some kind is often more appropriate for children since they are such physical creatures. They operate on a physical level and understand a physical sanction more easily.

Benedict is reluctant to use physical punishment. He understands that most people genuinely abhor physical discipline because of the suffering it causes children. But Benedict must also have realized that more often we turn away from using physical correction for more selfish reasons. Perhaps the use of smacks conflicts with our 'nice' self-image. More probably we don't like to take firm disciplinary action because we are too lazy and weak to confront the problem with the severity it deserves. Our weakness in this way spoils the child (Prov. 23.14). As Benedict says in chapter two, we must never overlook the faults of our children. We should treat their faults like poisonous weeds: 'Cut them out by the roots as soon as they begin to show themselves'.

If we heed Benedict's plan for discipline our use of corporal punishment will be rare, moderate and controlled. We should keep physical punishment as a last resort. The smacks should never be done in a moment of anger; instead, as Benedict recommends, there should be several warnings first. The warnings not only help the child, but they help us keep control. Most of all the motive for the smacks must never be our own desire to vent our anger. Instead, if we use corporal punishment, it must always be with utmost reluctance and because nothing else will heal the child's nature which has been wounded by sin.

CHAPTER XXXI
WHAT KIND OF MAN THE CELLARER OF THE MONASTERY SHOULD BE (A)

As cellarer of the monastery should be chosen from the community one who is sound in judgement, mature in character, sober, not a great eater, not self-important, not turbulent, not harshly spoken, not an off-putter, not wasteful, but a God-fearing man who will be a father to the whole community. He is to have charge of all affairs, but he is not to act without the Abbot's approval, and he must carry out his orders. He must not sadden the brethren. If any brother happens to make an unreasonable demand of him, he should not upset him by showing contempt, but refuse the ill-advised petitioner with reasons modestly presented. He must keep guard over his own soul, always bearing in mind that saying of the Apostle that he who has ministered well gains a good reputation for himself. With all compassion he is to have care for the sick, the children, the guests and the poor, knowing for certain that in the day of judgement he will have to render account for his treatment of them all. He must regard the chattels of the monastery and its whole property as if they were the sacred vessels of the altar. He should neglect nothing. He must neither succumb to avarice nor be a wasteful squanderer of the monastery's goods; but he should conduct all his affairs with prudence and in accordance with the Abbot's instructions.

The next section of the Rule deals with the physical administration of the monastery. As Benedict integrates the details of monastic services into his spiritual treatise, so he weaves the practical aspects of life into the Rule. Benedict's underlying assumption is that the physical and spiritual are united, and how we perform the ordinary tasks of life affect and reflect our spiritual condition.

As Esther de Waal points out, the characteristics required of the cellarer are the same as those St Paul lays down for a bishop in 1 Timothy 3.2–4. So the overseer of physical goods must resemble the spiritual overseer. Like the bishop, the administrator is one who serves (1 Tim. 3.13). It is easy to imagine that prayer and worship are more important than 'earthly' things. But for the Christian, 'matter matters'. As John of Damascus wrote, 'Since my Lord took matter and redeemed it, should I disdain matter?' As a result the cellarer is to regard the material goods of the monastery as if they were the sacred vessels of the altar. He must be a good steward, generous without being wasteful and thrifty without being stingy.

The cellarer is also called to be a good steward because physical things are the means by which he ministers to the needs of others. So he ministers carefully and diplomatically to his brothers, and uses the goods of the monastery to help the poor, children, the sick and guests to the monastery.

The cellarer's attitude to material wealth is a refreshing tonic in our consumerist society. In contrast to the cellarer, we are wasteful without being generous, and mean without being thrifty. We need to be good stewards of our own wealth and the world's resources because every gift from God is good (1 Tim. 4.4), and because the gifts of this material world are to be used not only for our own enjoyment, but to minister to the needy.

The first time this passage is read in the year is probably during Lent. So it is a good opportunity to re-examine our own attitude to material wealth, and how we are helping our children to become good stewards. Do we involve them in charity giving? Do we encourage a sharing and open-hearted attitude? Do we help them to save without being mean? Do we discourage waste? Are we teaching them to be aware of the larger issues of ecology and global poverty? If we cannot be good stewards of our earthly resources how can we be good stewards of our souls? (Luke 16.10–13).

CHAPTER XXXI
WHAT KIND OF MAN THE CELLARER OF THE MONASTERY SHOULD BE (B)

It is essential that he should have humility and if he has nothing material to give, he should at least offer a kind word of reply, as it is written, 'A good word surpasses the best gift.' He must keep under his own care whatever the Abbot has entrusted to him, but he should not undertake anything the Abbot has forbidden. He must provide the brethren with their regular allowance of food, without fuss or keeping them waiting, so as not to make for them an occasion of sin, keeping in mind the divine saying about the retribution of him 'who causes one of the little ones to sin.' If the community is rather large, helpers should be given him, so that with their aid he may himself tranquilly perform the office entrusted to him.

Whatever has to be asked for or given should be asked for or given at suitable times, so that no one may be upset or saddened in the household of God.

In the first section of this chapter Benedict points out that the cellarer is to be a 'godly father to the whole community'. So, like the abbot, the cellarer is an example for the Christian father. Today's reading shows that the cellarer's concern for the physical goods of the monastery is, at heart, a loving concern for the monks themselves. As the abbot takes care of their spiritual well-being, the cellarer is concerned with their physical needs. For Benedict the two roles are two aspects of the same loving concern.

If the cellarer hasn't anything to give, or needs to refuse a brother's request, then he must at least give him a kind reply. The cellarer is to provide for all the needs of the brothers fairly and on time so there is no occasion for grumbling. These details and the whole chapter are focused to one end: that 'no one may be upset or saddened in the household of God.'

The cellarer is an excellent icon of God the Father. He knows our needs before we ask (Matt. 6.8). He feeds the birds and clothes the lilies of the field, so he will provide all our physical needs at the right time (Matt. 6.25–34). As a result, Jesus teaches that we are not to worry, but to take one day at a time, trusting completely in God's providence. God, the great cellarer, will provide everything, so that no one in the household of God should be 'upset or saddened'.

The kind and quietly efficient cellarer also highlights our vocation as Christian fathers. We are to provide for our families with the same wise, mature and generous heart as that with which the cellarer provides for the monastery, and God provides for us. Whatever our job, it is not primarily to provide us with an interesting occupation, or a ladder to promotion and ever-increasing status. Instead, our work is the way we fulfil our primary vocation of providing for our family. In co-operation with our wife the day-to-day provision of physical food, clothing and shelter is also a spiritual vocation. Constructing a secure, loving and creative home provides the peace of mind children need for good spiritual health. A secure and abundant home life reflects the life of heaven, and as we mirror the cellarer in the home we also provide our children with an intimate – if imperfect – icon of God the Father.

CHAPTER XXXII
THE TOOLS AND GOODS OF THE MONASTERY

With regard to the monastery's material possessions such as tools, clothes, or other articles, the Abbot should put in charge of them brethren whose way of life and character he can trust, and then commit all these things to them, as he thinks best, for safe keeping, and return after use. The Abbot should keep a list of them so that when the brethren succeed one another in the tasks assigned to them he may know what is being handed over or received back. If anyone treats the property of the monastery in a dirty or careless manner, he should be corrected and if he does not amend, he should suffer punishment as laid down in the Rule.

☙

In the chapter on the cellarer Benedict says the material goods of the monastery must be treated as the sacred vessels of the altar. In this striking image he gives us his whole theology in a nutshell. The material world is sacred and we are to treat all things with reverence and love because they are pointers to the Creator. In today's chapter he reinforces this with practical rules for taking care of the material belongings of the monastery.

Underlying these guidelines is Benedict's strict rule against private ownership. In the monastery all things are held in common. Particular items are distributed as they are needed. Each tool, book, item of clothing or furniture is only lent to the monk. He is to be the steward of that item until it is returned to the abbot, and if it is returned dirty or broken he is to be disciplined. These practical details are important, not just as a matter of thrift, but because Benedict wants his monks to have a sacramental view of all material things.

Our society teaches us exactly the opposite view of the material world. It is to be raped, not reverenced. It is to be used and thrown away, not returned clean and whole. For us material things are to be grasped and owned, not given and lent. This attitude is rampant because mankind has forgotten his Creator, so the world is simply there to be exploited. The Christian attitude must be radically different. Our good cellarer, God the Father, has given us all good things to use wisely. Our wealth and possessions are not our own. They are only on loan. As a result we have a responsibility to use them carefully for the good of everyone in the community. This should also be our understanding of the whole world's resources.

So the Christian home is not a place of endless acquisition and personal hoarding. As with the monks, everything in the Christian home is held in common. And, as Benedict teaches, the details matter. So hand-me-down clothes and a shared toy cupboard convey truths about our proper relationship to the material world. Rooms should be kept tidy and toys and tools maintained not just because we are house-proud, but because these things matter. How we use a gift reflects our attitude to the giver; so if we despise and discard the gift we cannot pretend that we honour the giver.

CHAPTER XXXIII
WHETHER MONKS MAY HAVE PERSONAL PROPERTY

It is of the greatest importance that this vice should be totally eradicated from the monastery. No one may take it upon himself to give or receive anything without the Abbot's permission or to possess anything as his own, anything whatever, books or writing tablets or pen or anything at all; for they are not allowed to retain at their own disposition their own bodies or wills, but they must expect to receive all they need from the Father of the monastery. And so it must not be allowed that anyone should have anything which the Abbot has not approved. Everything should be common to all, as it is written, and no one should call anything his own or treat it as such. But if anyone is found to be entertaining this wicked vice, he should be warned once, and a second time; if he does not amend, he should undergo punishment.

❧

For the poor any little thing can become a treasure; so for the monk even a pen can be coveted. As a result, Benedict strictly roots out even the tiniest morsel of personal ownership. This seems harsh, but Benedict understands the gospel injunction that to enter the Kingdom and be perfect one has to sell everything and give to the poor (Matt. 19, 21; Mark. 10.21; Luke 12.33). He also understands that it is the poor who inherit the Kingdom of heaven (Matt. 5.3) and that it is difficult for the rich to enter (Matt. 19.23–24).

So in eradicating private ownership, Benedict forces the monks into an extreme personal poverty, and thus a complete reliance on the community and on God. Not owning anything – not even a pen – also allows the monk to exist on a plane of complete freedom and proper detachment from earthly things. Unlike the Franciscan, the Benedictine takes no vow of poverty. His personal poverty is balanced because he is able to enjoy the goods of the monastery. So the Benedictine's individual poverty integrates him more deeply with the community in a subtle interaction.

Private ownership is a necessary evil in society, but when it actually becomes the cornerstone of a civilization, things become horribly twisted. When private ownership becomes the be-all and end-all, our proper relationship with the material world is perverted. Our communities disintegrate because we have no need of others. Furthermore, our possession of something ultimately means someone else may not have it. The love of money is truly the root of all evil (1 Tim. 6.10), and in the Christian home we must be as radical as Benedict in rooting out the attitude of avarice which grows from the assumption of personal ownership. It is vital to develop an attitude of open-hearted sharing. If we have a large family it should not be too difficult because sharing becomes a necessity. Children in a large family simply cannot have a large hoard of personal property. Everything must be re-cycled, handed down and shared.

It is easy for a celibate monk to gather things to himself. He must force himself to live for the whole community. But in a large Christian family the monastic ideal of having all things in common becomes a joyful necessity. We should help everyone in the family to rejoice in this fact whenever they are tempted to 'hug good things to themselves'.

CHAPTER XXXIV
WHETHER ALL SHOULD
RECEIVE EQUAL SHARES

It is written, 'Distribution was made to each as he had need.' By this we do not say that favouritism should be shown to persons, far from it, but that infirmities should be allowed for. If someone needs less he should thank God and not be upset; if another needs more he should be humble about his weakness, and not feel important on account of the consideration shown him, and thus all members will be at peace. Above all the bad habit of grumbling must not make its appearance in any word or gesture for any reason whatever. If anyone is found guilty of this, let him pay a heavy penalty.

It is natural to equate fairness with equivalence. So we think that to be fair each person must be given the same amount of time, money and attention. But in the first Christian community goods were distributed according to need (Acts 4.35). Like the master in the parable of the talents (Matt. 25.14–30), the wise father gives to each of his children according to their ability (Matt. 25.15). When all were equally poor as a result of the rule forbidding private ownership, it might seem sensible to dole out equal rations to every monk, but Benedict recognizes that equality doesn't mean giving everyone the same amount, but giving everyone what they need.

Giving everyone the same is easy egalitarianism, but

such an approach eventually destroys peace. It makes people covet what others have because they think it is their 'right'. When this crude egalitarianism is linked with materialism the result is discontentment, and greed – then finally violence. Distributing according to need is far more challenging. It is challenging to the one distributing because he must be sensitive enough to determine each one's need. It is a challenge to those receiving because, by virtue of human nature, they will compare what they have been given with the person who has been given more, not the person who has received less. So the rule that good things are given according to need must be established and agreed by all.

Benedict forbids grumbling about this. Instead each monk should see that he has what he needs and be grateful. We should also cultivate this way of seeing God's provision for us. He gives according to need, not equally to all. Awareness of this will also help us distinguish between our needs and our wants. Once we have learned to see this, we should show our children that they receive everything they need, and so does everyone else in the family, and that there is a deeper and more caring fairness in this approach than simply giving the same amount to everyone.

This approach to sharing curbs greed and envy, while it encourages contentment and sensitivity to one another's unique set of gifts and needs. The wise *abba*, in the monastery or the home, uses the gifts of one to fulfil the needs of another so that each person is fulfilled by giving and receiving. So the Christian community is not a hive of drones but a body of love.

CHAPTER XXXV
THE WEEKLY SERVERS IN THE KITCHEN (A)

The brethren should serve one another, and no one should be excused from kitchen duty except for sickness or because he is more usefully engaged elsewhere, because through this service the reward of an increase in charity is gained. For the weak, however, help should be provided so that this duty may not cause them dejection. Indeed all should have help according to the size of the community and the location. If the community is rather large the cellarer should be excused from kitchen duty and, as we said before, also those who are engaged in more important tasks. The rest should serve one another in turn with charity. The one who is finishing his week's duty does the washing on the Saturday; he should also wash the towels with which the brethren dry their hands and feet. Moreover, he who is ending his week's service together with him who is about to start should wash the feet of all. The outgoing server must restore the crockery he has made use of, washed and intact to the cellarer, and the cellarer must hand it over to the incomer, so that he knows what he is giving out and what he is getting back.

No detail is too small for Benedict to integrate it into the spirituality of the monastery. In this chapter the matter of kitchen chores becomes a living image of the servanthood of Christ himself. As the monk serves his brothers at table he is reminded that Christ came among us as one who serves (Luke 22.27), and that he did not consider equality with God something to be grasped, but took the form of a servant (Phil. 2.7). As the servant is not above his master, we are to do the same (Matt. 20.26–28).

In a moving detail Benedict says the outgoing kitchen server and the one taking up his duties are to wash the feet of the other monks when the duties change over at the beginning of the week. This links the kitchen chores with the Last Supper when Jesus took a towel and washed the disciples' feet. (John 13.4–5); so service in the refectory is almost sacramentally linked with the Eucharist and the Easter mystery. All the more reason for the crockery, the linens and the cutlery to be handled with care, attention and devotion.

This chapter touches and challenges our own lives in two ways. Firstly, what is our attitude to our daily work? Can we see any element of service, or is it simply a daily grind of constant competition and pressure to deliver? If we can see service to others within our work then it begins to have a deeper meaning. As Benedict has 'redeemed' kitchen drudgery we may be able to gather a sense of vocation out of a job which we thought was meaningless.

There is a further application for our home life. Benedict makes it clear that the monks' opportunity of service is immediately to hand in the community where he lives. Each meal is a chance for service, and each brother is a person to be served. Is this the attitude in our family life? At that crunch time between 4 p.m. and 8 p.m. when everyone is tired, hungry and irritable, are we there to be served or to serve? The children should also be involved. Benedict's instructions that no one should be excused completely, and that the weak should receive help, remind us that even young children can help around the house. If chores are shared they are more fun, and children can also understand that household tasks have a deeper meaning. Jesus served others, so we should too.

March 14
July 14
November 13

CHAPTER XXXV
THE WEEKLY SERVERS IN THE KITCHEN (B)

*An hour before the meal, the weekly servers may each receive, in
addition to the allotted quantity, a drink and some bread, so that
at the hour of the meal they may serve their brethren without
finding the work heavy or complaining. On solemn days,
however, they must wait for the Mass. On Sundays, immediately after Lauds, the incoming and outgoing servers should
prostrate themselves at the feet of all the brethren in the oratory,
and ask to be prayed for. The outgoing server is to say the verse,
'Blessed are you Lord God for you have helped and strengthened
me.' When this has been said three times, and he has received a
blessing, the incoming server follows and says, 'O God come to
my aid, Lord make haste to help me.' And this too is to be
repeated three times by all. And so, having received the blessing,
he begins his week's duty.*

In a typical touch, Benedict allows for the kitchen servers
to have a special ration of food so they won't get hungry
and grumpy while serving others. This kind of foresight
and planning of detail is for the smooth running of the
monastery and also for the welfare of the monks serving.
Once more, in addition to the practical details, Benedict
weaves in the spiritual dimension. The incoming server
says the prayer which starts each Office: 'O God come to
my assistance; O Lord make haste to help me'. The out-

going server says, 'Blessed are you Lord God for you have helped and strengthened me', then asks for a blessing. This formality brings the words and actions of the chapel into the refectory so that the whole monastic life has an inner consistency and unity.

This should be our aim as well. One of the stresses of modern life is that it is so fragmented. The world of work exists separately from our home life, our hobbies, our children's school community and our church. Furthermore, the different elements of our lives often tend to conflict and compete for our attention. We need discipline to integrate the fragmented segments of life. A rule helps us to order our priorities, and prayer can be the thread which strings all the different dimensions together.

Benedict sanctifies kitchen duties by integrating an element of ritual and prayer into the heart of the service. So we can develop our own rituals and prayers within the context of a busy professional and home life. The family can start a car journey with a prayer for safety which recognizes that we are on a spiritual journey through life. Grace at the beginning of a meal can become a small ritual which not only thanks God for food, but refers us on to consider the eucharistic feast. Arrow prayers for help when we are stressed or in some need can become a ritual which blesses an activity and integrates it into a more whole vision of our lives.

This ritualistic dimension to life is especially appropriate for children. They love order, set rules and routine. So in family prayer establish places to sit, set gestures and routine words which make the prayers into a small liturgy. Repeating the same prayers at fixed times thus sanctifies the daily routine and drudgery and repetitious tasks become actions of prayer and loving service.

CHAPTER XXXVI
SICK BRETHREN

The care of the sick is to be given priority over everything else, so that they are indeed served as Christ would be served, since he said of himself, 'I was sick and you visited me,' and 'What you did to one of the least, you did to me.' But the sick themselves must realise that it is to pay honour to God that they are being served, and they must not vex their brethren by asking for too much. However, they must be borne with patience, because through them a very ample recompense is merited. Therefore let the Abbot pay the greatest attention so that they suffer no neglect.

For the sick brethren a separate room must be provided, and to serve them a brother who is God-fearing, diligent and zealous. the use of baths should be allowed to the sick as often as is desirable, but to the healthy and the young this should not be granted very often. Moreover, the eating of meat should be allowed to the sick who are in a weak condition, but when they are restored to health again, all should abstain from meat as usual. The Abbot must take the greatest care that the sick are not neglected by the cellarer or those who serve them, for whatever is done wrong by his disciples concerns him.

~

Benedict moves from service in the kitchen to service in the sick bay. He goes directly to the gospels and affirms that in serving the sick we serve Christ himself, for what we do for one of the least we do for him (Matt. 25.36–40). This is a primary Christian duty, but Benedict doesn't teach it in an abstract way. As usual the duty to care for the sick is there within the community itself, and this hands-on approach requires attention to isolation wards, bath times, diet and alteration of the regime. In later Benedictine life, of course, the monastery was the primary source of health care for the whole population, and the monks developed extensive medical skills.

Our own response to the sick is ambiguous. On the one hand, we enjoy the best nutrition and health care ever, but on the other hand, because of the media, we are more aware of the sick, starving and suffering in the world than ever before. So it is important that we give and get involved in international relief work; but Benedict would also insist that we get involved at ground level. We don't have to look far to discover the sick, the housebound, the prisoners or the disadvantaged in our society. It is only when we get involved with real people and real circumstances that our service of Christ in our neighbour begins in earnest. So Mother Teresa used to advise people: 'Do not come out to help me in Calcutta. Find the sick, the poor and the lonely who live near you.'

Ministering to the sick with a visit or a gift is an excellent way to introduce our children to the whole area of suffering. It won't be pleasant for them to visit someone who is sick or dying, but being confronted with the grim reality will help to widen their experience in life. They will see what hard work it is to care for the sick. They will also understand how prayer, caring and love help to heal the sick. Then when they are faced with suffering in their own lives they will not be shocked because they have not been overly protected. Ministering to the sick and suffering will provide the tools they need to redeem the evil and bring light out of the darkness.

CHAPTER XXXVII
OLD MEN AND CHILDREN

Although human nature itself is drawn to feel sympathy for those in these stages of life, namely the old and children, yet it is right that the authority of the Rule also should have regard to them. Their weaknesses should at all times be taken into consideration, and the letter of the Rule should by no means be applied to them in matters of food. Indeed they should always be thought of compassionately, and they should have their meals before the prescribed times.

It is part of human nature to have a special fondness and concern for children and old people. Elsewhere Benedict uses food as a disciplinary tool; here he uses it to show special concern for the needs of the elderly and the very young. One is hungry because he is growing fast. The other can't wait for food because he is weak with age. Both are given special consideration, and it is this principle of caring for the 'useless' members of society which makes Benedict's rule so civilized.

Benedict's gentle civility implies a sharp comment on our harsh modern attitudes. He assumes that we all have a gentle love for the young and the elderly. Not necessarily in our society. Too often we regard the elderly as a burden and the young as a nuisance. This attitude is the fruit of the 'culture of death' which has developed. When children are killed in the womb, why should we value children outside the womb? When unproductive people are suddenly sacked from their jobs after a lifetime's service, why should we be surprised when the elderly are considered a costly burden? As euthanasia comes galloping in hard on the heels of abortion, Benedict's gentle advice to have special consideration for the young and the elderly makes our society look barbaric and primitive.

As fathers, husbands, and sons we are faced with extremely difficult decisions. Should we allow the culture of death to infiltrate our own lives by artificially closing the door to more children? Would we ever contemplate abortion as a solution to an unwanted pregnancy? Have we made plans for looking after our parents as they grow older? How do we regard those who are weak, vulnerable and 'useless' in our community? Benedict has already reminded us that how we treat 'the least of these' is how we treat Christ himself (Matt. 25.40).

Our response to these questions will influence our children's understanding of the faith. When children reach the age of early puberty they are ruthless at sniffing out hypocrisy and humbug. If they hear us profess a religion of compassion, but see only a selfish denial of life, they will conclude that our religion was only so much pious talk, and if they leave the practice of their faith it will be our responsibility too. For causing them to stumble our Lord has sombre warnings (Luke 17.2).

CHAPTER XXXVIII
THE WEEKLY READER

At the meals of the brethren there should always be reading, but not by anyone who happens to take up the book. There shall be a reader for the whole week, and he is to begin on Sunday. Let him begin after Mass and Communion by asking the prayers of all that God may keep from him the spirit of vanity. The reader himself is to intone the verse, **O Lord open my lips, and my mouth shall proclaim your praise,** *and it is to be said three times by all. And so, having received a blessing, let him begin to read. There is to be complete silence, so that no whisper nor any voice other than that of the reader be heard there. Whatever is wanted for eating and drinking the brethren should pass to one another, so that no one need ask for anything. If, however, something is wanted, it should be asked for by some sign or sound rather than by speaking. No one there present is to ask any question about the reading or about anything, so that no opportunity for disturbance may arise; unless perhaps the superior wishes to say a few words for edification. The weekly reader may take some refreshment before he begins to read because of his Holy Communion and lest his fast should be a burden to him. He is to take his meal afterwards with the weekly cooks and servers.*

The brethren are not to read (or sing) in their order of seniority but only those who edify the listeners.

❧

One of the most surprising and delightful things one notices on a first visit to a monastery is the silence and formality at mealtime. The monks stand to chant a Latin grace. The servers stand at attention while the portion of Scripture is read. Then at a sign from the abbot they serve the meal according to an established order. As Benedict says in today's reading, 'If something is wanted, it should be asked for by some sign or sound rather than by speaking'. 'There is to be complete silence, so that no whisper nor any voice other than that of the reader be heard there.'

What is important here is not so much that the meal is eaten in silence, but that the meal is undertaken with an almost courtly etiquette and ritual. This formalized approach to mealtime takes us aback because the civility of our own mealtimes has disintegrated almost completely. Too often the busy pace of life and availability of fast food means we grab food and eat it on the run, or each individual in a family 'grazes', taking whatever food strikes their fancy as and when they see fit. Even if we do sit down to a family meal the manners are often poor and the conversation is non-existent. We are missing out on one of the cornerstones of civilized society – the fellowship meal.

To counter this we needn't take meals in silence, but we can certainly mark festive times with a formal meal. We can also establish at least one meal at week, probably Sunday lunch, as a formal family meal. We can work together to plan a good menu, use decent cutlery and crockery, stand for grace, practise good table and conversational manners and finish the ritual with another grace thanking God for those who have prepared the meal. The Benedictine silence could be established by keeping a moment's silence after the grace. The Benedictine custom of reading could include taking a moment to read a short, appropriate psalm or passage about the particular festival we are celebrating.

The monks maintain a ceremonial meal because it links mealtime with the greater ceremony which takes place in church. The formal communal meal thus becomes another aspect to the integrated life of worship and prayer. So too for our family, treating a meal in a ceremonious manner not only helps the children develop decent social skills, but it points beyond that meal to the Eucharist and the eternal banquet in heaven.

CHAPTER XXXIX

THE MEASURE OF FOOD

We consider it to be enough for the daily meal, whether at the sixth or the ninth hour, that there should always be served two cooked dishes, to allow for the weaknesses of different eaters; so that if someone cannot eat of the one dish he may still make a meal from the other. So two cooked dishes should be enough for all the brethren. And if fruit or tender vegetables are to be had, a third dish may be added. A full pound of bread should be enough for a day, whether there is one meal or those of dinner and supper. If there is a supper a third of the pound of bread should be kept back by the cellarer and produced at that meal.

If, however, their work is rather heavy, it will be in the Abbot's power and in his judgement to decide whether it is expedient to increase the allowance. But there must be no danger of over-eating, so that no monk is overtaken by indigestion, for there is nothing so opposed to Christian life as over-eating, as our Lord says, 'Take care that your hearts are not weighed down by over-eating.' Young boys should not be given the same amount of food, but less than their elders. Frugality should be the rule on all occasions. All must refrain entirely from eating the flesh of quadrupeds, except for the sick who are really weak.

Nothing is too small for Benedict to comment on. He is well aware that proper attention to food keeps a community or family hearty, healthy and happy. He understands that food affects mood. So to avoid grumbling he provides for a choice of dishes for those who are fussy while allowing plenty of bread for those who are always hungry. He encourages fresh fruit and vegetables. There is to be no over-eating and no red meat. This is reminiscent of the healthy diet which Daniel requested for himself and his friends when they found themselves in the Babylonian court (Dan. 1.11–13).

Benedict takes time to deal with food in detail because he is always concerned to integrate the physical aspect of life with the spiritual quest. Food is the one physical thing which we actually eat and make a part of us. Both good nutrition and fasting affect our bodies and therefore affect our spiritual condition. Furthermore, Benedict advises moderation in food matters because extreme attitudes about food indicate and encourage the wrong spiritual responses. The one who is greedy at table is exhibiting and indulging his selfish love of pleasure. The one who is over-fastidious shows a sour and negative attitude, which is another form of self-centredness.

But attention to food is also important because it takes us to the basic level of life. Benedict and his monks would have grown or gathered most of their own food. They knew the value of food. As a hard-won commodity it required careful stewardship and distribution. In our consumerist society we have forgotten how to value food properly. We take for granted the enormous amount and variety of food which is available. Supermarkets isolate us from the real human cost of producing that food, and from the seasonal or local aspect to food. As a result food has become a mass-produced consumer item and we see no link between what we eat and what we are. Saying grace at meal times is a small way to help restore the balance. It helps us and our families to remember the value of food, to remember those who are hungry and to be grateful. Cultivating the proper response to particular physical things influences the way we see the whole physical realm, and, as Benedict keeps reminding us, the way we treat the physical creation is a reflection of our attitude to the Creator himself.

March 19
July 19
November 18

CHAPTER XL
THE MEASURE OF DRINK

'Each man has his special gift from God, one of one kind, another of another kind,' and hence it is with some diffidence that we fix the quantity of the food and drink of others. But keeping in view the frailty of the weak, we think that half a pint of wine daily is enough for each. Those, however, to whom God grants the capacity to abstain should know that they will have their own reward.

If, however, local conditions or their work or the summer heat call for more, it must be for the superior to decide, but he must take care that neither excess nor drunkenness overtakes them. For although we read that wine is not at all a drink for monks, yet, since in our days it is impossible to persuade monks of this, let us agree at least about this that we should not drink our fill, but more sparingly, since 'wine leads even wise men into infidelity.'

When, however, local conditions bring it about that the above mentioned quantity is not available, but much less, or none at all, then those who live there should bless God and not grumble. We lay special stress on this that the brethren remain free from grumbling.

Some translations say a half-bottle of wine is sufficient each day. But then the natural question is, 'How big is the bottle?' Benedict is rightly hesitant to legislate about the specific amount of wine that can be drunk. As he says, 'Every man has a special gift from God' (1 Cor. 7.7). For some a half-bottle is too much, for others a half-bottle is not enough. The principle here is that Benedict does not wish to legislate at all if laying down a rule means complete prohibition. He recognizes with St Paul that all things are good and are to be received with thanksgiving (1 Tim. 4.4).

At the same time he recognizes that wine is a bit of a luxury and has its dangers. If a monk can abstain completely that is a good thing, and if a monk is in such a time and place that wine is unavailable he mustn't consider it a right or allow it to be a cause for grumbling. Here, as always with Benedict, we are getting beyond the particular physical thing to consider the state of mind and heart which Benedict is trying to cultivate.

Within ourselves and amongst our families we must cultivate a proper attitude to the luxuries of life. First of all we must distinguish between our needs and our wants. We are very quick to see pleasurable wants as needs and very loath to recognize unpleasant needs as necessary at all. So for the child chocolates become necessary and vegetables an optional extra. We do the same thing with things we like and dislike. Instead we must work to develop a mature understanding of our needs. This will lead to a proper relationship with the luxuries of life.

Benedict isn't a Puritan. He wants us to enjoy the luxuries, but he is cautious. We should avoid treating them as our right to such an extent that we grumble if they become unavailable. So we also need to encourage our children to enjoy life's pleasures but never to consider them as necessities. To do so devalues both the luxuries and everything else. Becoming addicted to luxuries – whether it is television, gambling or chocolate – is a bit like being drunk. We lose our perspective, our senses become dulled, and our spiritual vision becomes blurred because we have become addicted to a lesser good. Instead Benedict advises moderation in all things.

CHAPTER XLI
AT WHAT HOURS THEY SHOULD TAKE THEIR MEALS

From the holy feast of Easter until Pentecost the brethren are to have their dinner at midday, and their supper in the evening. From Pentecost throughout the summer, unless the monks have work in the fields or the summer is oppressively hot, they should fast on Wednesdays and Fridays until the ninth hour, and on the other days have dinner at midday; but the midday meal may be kept up continuously throughout the week, if they have work in the fields or the summer heat is excessive; it will be for the Abbot to decide. For he is to modify and organise all their affairs in such wise that their souls may be saved, and that the brethren do whatever they do, without justification for grumbling.

From 14 September, however, until the beginning of Lent they should always have their meal at the ninth hour.

During Lent until Easter it should be in the evening.

Vespers, however, should be sung at such an hour that the brethren will not need lamp-light for their meal, but that everything will be finished by daylight. Indeed at all seasons, the hour of supper or of the evening meal should be calculated so that everything may be done by daylight.

☙

It might seem that Benedict is caught up in trivia in taking a whole chapter to regulate mealtimes. But this attention to detail not only helps order institutional life, but it also helps keep the monks from grumbling. Men like to know when the food is arriving, so Benedict takes time to make sure everyone knows where they stand. In regulating mealtimes, Benedict also regulates the fasting required of the monks.

Fasting on Wednesdays and Fridays is an ancient and venerable custom. Fasting, like all forms of asceticism, is never to be used because the physical world is sinful. Instead, Benedict – always aware of the spiritual battle and the spiritual race to be won – would recommend fasting as a form of training for the spiritual soldier and athlete. So we fast to control our physical appetite. We fast to feel healthier and more alert. Fasting helps us discover just what controls us most. Are we controlled by our physical hunger or our spiritual hunger? Fasting helps make us more aware of our need for God. We may also fast to identify more with the plight of the poor and to make a personal sacrifice for others.

In all of this, either eating or not eating, Benedict reminds us yet again that our bodies and souls are interrelated, and what happens to one affects the other profoundly. This is why, after he recommends fasting, he also advises on various situations where fasting is not appropriate. If the monks are working hard in the summer sun, fasting will only make them weak and irritable. Far from turning their minds to God, the fast in such conditions will only make them think of food even more.

Fasting has a proper place in the Christian home too. International aid charities often organize a 'family fast day' which focuses attention on the needy in developing countries. We should take part. The season of Lent is a chance to practise all sorts of creative ways to 'fast'. Sacrificing one thing in order to take on a positive activity helps children make sense of fasting. Fasting in the family should not be an onerous duty. God loves a cheerful giver (Matt. 6.16). Nevertheless there is always a more serious side to fasting. So giving up meat on Fridays reminds us of Christ's sacrifice on Good Friday. All of us need time to reflect on the more sombre aspects of life and a Friday fast gives space for this to happen.

CHAPTER XLII
THAT NO ONE MAY SPEAK AFTER COMPLINE

At all times monks ought to strive to keep silence but particularly so during the hours of the night, and this means in all seasons, whether on days of fasting or on days of having a midday meal.

If it is the latter season, then after rising from supper, they should at once sit together and one of them should read the **Conferences** *or the* **Lives of the Fathers** *or some other work which will edify the hearers, but not the Heptateuch or the Books of Kings; for this part of Scripture will not be helpful to those of weaker intelligence at this hour; they should, however, be read at some other time.*

If it has been a fast day, then after Vespers there will be a short interval, and then they should assemble for the reading of the **Conferences** *as we have said. Four or five pages should be read, or as many as the time permits; and during this space of time for reading all come together, including anyone who may have been occupied in a job assigned to him.*

So when all are assembled, they should say Compline, and when they come out of Compline there should be no further permission for anyone to talk about anything. If anyone is found transgressing this rule of silence he is to be punished severely, unless the need to attend to guests has arisen, or it happens that the Abbot has given someone an order. And in this case, too, the matter is to be handled with all seriousness and genuine moderation.

Benedict's monks slept when it was dark and rose with the dawn. So for them the natural rhythms of darkness and light were deeply significant. Darkness was the time of evil, and Compline consisted not only of prayers before sleep, but prayers for protection and strength to battle with the spiritual powers of darkness (Eph. 6.12). So Benedict equips his monks to enter the darkness or 'the Great Silence'. After supper they are to read from Cassian's *Conferences* or the *Lives of the Desert Fathers* – two books of monastic wisdom. Then after Compline silence reigns supreme. Silence is commanded because the battle takes place in the dark recesses of the heart, and conversation distracts.

The monks certainly got up while it was still dark to 'do battle' in the office of Vigils, but Benedict was also aware that the 'battle' went on during sleep as well. We know sleep restores us physically and mentally, but sleep should also be a time for spiritual rejuvenation. If we ask God to work in our lives during sleep, the Spirit can hover over the darkness of our souls and do a creative and healing work within. Furthermore, through the natural therapy of sleep God can bring to mind hidden traumas from the past. Once they surface they can be put under his forgiving love. So good sleep provides good health in body, mind and spirit. This requires proper preparation. As Benedict advises the monks to share some holy reading and then say Compline together, so we should examine what we do with our time before bed. Do we stay up to watch violent, lust-inspiring and mindless rubbish on television? Instead we should devote the time to some serious reading, then finish the day with Compline. An excellent way to do this is to light some candles and play a disc of some monks singing the Office of Compline, and so enter into the peaceful spirit of the ancient night Office.

Children also sleep better if they are prepared spiritually for bedtime. Prayers before sleep help them to review the day and bring their concerns to God. It is an intimate time when they are open to love and be loved in God's presence. Prayers for good sleep help keep our children sound in body, mind and spirit. So proper preparation for the 'Great Silence' is a moving and powerful conclusion of the day for the whole family.

CHAPTER XLIII
LATECOMERS TO THE WORK OF GOD OR TO MEALS (A)

As soon as the signal for the Divine Office is heard, the brethren must leave whatever they have been engaged in doing, and hasten with all speed; but with dignity, so that foolishness finds no stimulus. Nothing, therefore, is to be given preference over the Work of God.

*If at the Night Office anyone arrives after the **Glory be** of Psalm 94, which for this reason we wish to be said altogether slowly and deliberately, he must not stand in his place in the choir, but last of all, or in a place set apart by the Abbot for such careless persons, so that they may be seen by the Abbot and by everyone else, until at the end of the Work of God he does penance by public satisfaction. We have thought it best that such persons should stand last or else apart, so that being shamed because they are noticed by everybody, they may for this motive mend their ways. For if they stay outside the oratory, there may be someone who will go back and go to sleep again, or maybe sit down outside the oratory and give himself up to gossip, and in this way an opportunity is given to the evil one; it is better that they go in and not lose the benefit of the whole Office: and they should mend their ways as well.*

*At the Day Hours anyone who has not arrived at the Work of God after the versicle and the **Glory be** of the first Psalm that follows it, must take the last place as we have laid down above, nor may he take for granted permission to join the choir as they*

sing, until he has made satisfaction, unless the Abbot pardons
him and gives him permission; nevertheless one guilty of this
fault should still make satisfaction.

As soon as it is time for prayer the monk downs tools and
heads for the chapel. There is evidence in some medieval
manuscripts that monks would stop copying even in the
middle of a word to get up for the Office. But with a
typical gentle touch Benedict advises that the first psalm
be said slowly to allow time for latecomers to hurry in
without a punishment. The whole chapter is designed not
only to nurture efficiency in the community, but also to
help the monks establish their priorities. So Benedict sums
up the whole chapter: 'Nothing, therefore, is to be given
preference over the Work of God'.

We do well to have set times of prayer and stick to them.
Instead of saying we will pray 'some time in the evening'
we should pick an hour we can manage, and when that
moment comes we should keep our appointment with the
Lord. This element of routine is not only a useful discipline, it aids the prayer itself. Just as the body becomes
attuned to a routine and becomes hungry at certain times,
so the soul becomes used to its time of prayer. After
keeping a set prayer time for only a few weeks we will
soon notice the soul beginning to settle down and expect
that spiritual nourishment and communion with God. If
we do not set a time for prayer this beautiful instinct will
never develop. So it is that the monastic tradition and the
whole tradition of 'the prayer of the church' sets great
weight on appointing certain times for prayer and keeping
to them.

The same thing applies to our family prayers. Children
love routine because they know where they stand. It gives
a sense of order and security to their lives. So a set time for
a morning prayer and an evening prayer is essential. A
favourite memorized prayer helps make the routine
secure while informal extemporaneous prayer provides
variety and spontaneity. At the same time it is part of the

Benedictine ethos to be flexible. No routine for ourselves or our family must be too rigid. The principle is that 'nothing should come before the work of God'. The practice is that sometimes the Work of God will be most valued if it is placed at a different time which better suits the changing pattern of family life.

CHAPTER XLIII
LATECOMERS TO THE WORK OF GOD OR TO MEALS (B)

With regard to meals, the brother who does not arrive before the verse, so that all may say the verse and pray together and go to their meal together, that is the brother who does not arrive either through carelessness or other fault, should be admonished twice for this behaviour. If then he does not amend, he will not be permitted to share the common meal, but will be separated from the companionship of the others to eat alone, and will be deprived of his portion of wine, until he makes satisfaction and improves. The same applies to anyone who absents himself from the verse said after the meal.

Moreover, no one should be so bold as to take any food or drink before or after the regular meal time. But if something is offered to a brother by the superior and he rejects it, then when he does want what he previously rejected, or something else, he is not to receive anything at all until he makes suitable satisfaction.

୭

Benedict is careful to teach the monks good manners. They are to come on time to the communal meals. They are to accept what they are given and be grateful. Once again, efficient running of the monastery is not the only motive. Benedict wants the monks to learn that lateness and bad manners are actually inconsiderate towards others. That is why his punishment is for the monk to be isolated from the communal meal. If he can't behave like a responsible community member he is to be separated from the community.

Any parent who organizes meal times will recognize the same tension. The meal is prepared, children are bellowed for and there is no response. When they do come trailing in they respond to the food either with a fussy turned-up nose or with greedy grabbing. These bad manners are the fruit of an inner selfishness and ingratitude, and that is why they should be stamped out. Family mealtime is a vital opportunity naturally to train children in consideration for others, sharing and gratitude for what has been provided. If our family life disintegrates to individual meals taken in front of the television, it means we can't be bothered to teach the simple good manners which mark a civilized person – one who has learned to control himself because he lives in community with others.

The lack of simple courtesy and good manners indicates a selfish, arrogant and crude individual, and this has spiritual ramifications. Spiritual growth can never happen if the most basic faults are not remedied. Not even the simplest peasant saint had bad manners. For bad manners are, in the final analysis, disrespect and unconcern for others. Likewise punctuality is a form of keeping one's word. When we are late we waste not only our own time, but that of everyone else who waits for us as well. Punctuality and good manners are also a sign of maturity. The egocentric animal has become aware of the existence of others, and has begun to respond with sensitivity, keeping in mind that we should always treat others as we wish to be treated ourselves.

Finally, punctuality and good manners indicate a spiritual state of awareness. We are not so absorbed in our own interests and appetites that we fail to see the simple needs of others. This is a first step towards holiness, and children especially need to be trained to have good manners that become automatic.

CHAPTER XLIV
HOW THE EXCOMMUNICATED ARE TO MAKE SATISFACTION

If, for serious faults, anyone is excommunicated from the oratory and from the common meals, he is to lie prostrate at the threshold of the oratory at the time when the Work of God is being carried out, saying nothing, but just lying there with his head to the ground at the feet of them all as they come out of the oratory. This he is to continue to do until the Abbot considers the satisfaction to be enough. When at the Abbot's bidding he comes in, he must cast himself at the feet of the Abbot and then at the feet of the others, that they may pray for him. Then following the Abbot's instructions he may be admitted into choir, in such position as the Abbot decides, but on condition that he does not presume to sing alone any Psalm or reading or anything else, until the Abbot gives a fresh order. Moreover, at every hour, when the Work of God is being finished, he is to cast himself on the ground in the place where he is standing. And so must continue to do penance, until the Abbot again orders him to stop making this satisfaction.

With regard to those who for less serious faults are excommunicated from meals only, they are to make satisfaction in the oratory until the Abbot orders them to stop. They perform this penance until the Abbot gives his blessing and says, 'That is enough.'

☙

Benedict recognizes that a fault in community is a sin against each member of the community, so he demands public humiliation. The monk is to prostrate himself before his brethren until the abbot releases him. The main reason for this harsh treatment is to root out the pride which does not allow the monk to admit he has made a mistake. Not being able to admit sin in our lives is the most basic stumbling-block to spiritual progress.

The most subtle form of this pride presents itself as false humility. This appears in what we call 'a poor self-image'. Very often the person who thinks they are ugly, stupid or no good will also never admit to sin in their lives. They deny real responsibility for sin, but don't think they are proud because they are always telling themselves how terrible they are. The sin is excused with the comment, 'I'm only human, after all'. This is a twisted attitude. God expects us to 'love ourselves' on the one hand (Matt. 19.19), but also to acknowledge our sin before him (Ps. 51.3). Another form of self-deception is the psychological theory which seeks to blame others for our sins. So our sins are caused by our environment, our upbringing, our circumstances or the company we keep. Benedict will have none of this, and his harsh treatment of the offender is his way of insisting that the monk face his crime.

Esther de Waal points out that in prostrating himself the offender has to come literally face to face with the earth. So he symbolically comes face to face with himself, for from the dust of the earth he has come and will return. This lays down a good principle for proper discipline in the home. Not only should the punishment suit the crime, but it should also help the child face up to what he has done, and face up to himself. So if a child is isolated for bad behaviour he or she might write an essay or story about what they have done, or why it was wrong. If they are younger they might draw a picture of the person they hurt with their bad behaviour.

Most of all, Benedict wants us to take responsibility for our actions. From the very first words of the Prologue he has called us to make an active decision, to engage our wills and take responsibility for our souls' destination. We can only do this as we faithfully examine our consciences and with true repentance run in the path of God's commandments.

CHAPTER XLV
ON THOSE WHO MAKE MISTAKES IN THE ORATORY

If anyone goes wrong in giving out a Psalm, responsory, antiphon or reading, unless by making satisfaction he humbles himself there before all, he must submit to greater punishment; for he refused to put right with humility what he did wrong through lack of care. And boys should be beaten for such a fault.

In the stricter Benedictine monasteries, if you watch carefully while the monks are singing the Office you will sometimes see a particular monk step out of his stall briefly, bow to the abbot and then to his brothers. Without interrupting the flow of the liturgy the abbot will nod, the brother will then return to his stall and resume his place in the divine praises. The monk has committed some error or oversight in his singing of the Office, and, following the Rule literally, he has immediately humbled himself before all.

Benedict is establishing the principle that when there is a public crime there should be a public recompense. So in the rough-and tumble of family life, when there is open wrongdoing it is healthy for everyone to ask forgiveness openly and instantly. This is because a public fault injures all those who witness it, even if they are not personally involved. This is especially true when parents fight in front of the children. The effect on the children is profound, and often far greater than the dispute warrants from an adult perspective. So Benedict's ruling that forgiveness for a public fault should be open and instantaneous is very wise. In practical terms, if the children see us quarrel they should also see us ask forgiveness. If they experience the wrong they should also experience the reconciliation.

This instant admission of fault and instant reconciliation is not easy. We prefer to carry the grievance with us, giving ourselves time to justify our actions. But Benedict says those who don't admit their wrongdoing and seek immediate reconciliation should receive a more severe punishment. In this he is simply observing a natural law, for if we carry the grievance in our hearts we will indeed receive a more severe punishment: the punishment of accumulated stress, bitterness and permanently wounded relationships.

His brief word about boys being smacked is another reminder that sometimes a short, sharp physical punishment is most effective for children. If it is truly done in love not anger, then it speaks with its own inner logic. But there is more to this than simply condoning corporal punishment. Within the context Benedict is acknowledging that a child can rarely take the mature step of acknowledging his own wrongdoing and seeking reconciliation instantly. The physical punishment from the child's father is an objective outside corrective. It brings him up short and helps him see that part of growing up is admitting one's own fault and taking the initiative to set things right.

CHAPTER XLVI
ON THOSE WHO COMMIT FAULTS IN ANY OTHER MATTERS

If anyone while engaged in his work, in the kitchen, in the cellarer's offices, in the storeroom, in the bakery, in the garden or while engaged in any craft, or indeed anywhere else, behaves badly or breaks some article or destroys it, or commits some excess, he should come straightaway before the Abbot and the community, declare his transgression and make satisfaction. But if he does not do this, and the transgression becomes known through another, he must undergo a heavier penalty.

However, if the failing be an interior sin, he should declare it only to the Abbot or to spiritual fathers, for they, knowing how to heal their own wounds, know how to heal those of others, without revealing them or making them known.

Our first human instinct is to conceal our wrongdoing. But Benedict allows no room for this basic cowardice and pride. If a fault occurs, if a monk loses or breaks anything, he must come forward on his own or suffer more severe punishment.

But Benedict once more shows his wisdom and compassion; as this fault is not public it does not require public humiliation and reconciliation. The guilty party can simply come in private to the abbot, admit his fault and make restitution. This is practical and profound, and provides a simple rule for similar problems within a Christian family.

But as usual Benedict is touching on more than simple
breakages and lost property. He probes deeper to the
inner faults which prey on the monk's conscience. These
too may be brought quietly to the abbot, for in his wisdom
the abbot 'knows how to heal his own wounds and the
wounds of others'. This points to the healing which is
offered in the beautiful sacrament of reconciliation.

Likewise with our children, the inner faults are far more
serious and important than outward problems. It is touching to realize that whenever he refers to the inner condition Benedict never speaks in terms of 'severe
punishment' but only of healing. With inner faults there is
no place for severity, only compassion and mercy. Benedict knows that we treat ourselves too leniently in
outward matters while being too hard on ourselves as
regards the inner life.

The quick admission of outward faults helps re-estab-
lish a proper perspective. A wise father will therefore help
his children to pick up the outer faults quickly while
showing that unconditional love which gives them a positive and confident self-image. Establishing this delicate
balance within each child is an art and a grace which
requires tact, listening and tenderness, and it is best done
by both parents working in a complementary manner.

The inner life of even the youngest child is a marvel-
lously complex universe. Children are vulnerable. As they
reach adolescence their inner problems can become sore
points, and they will not want anyone probing. Establishing and keeping the trust of our children is no mean task.
We can only hope to win their trust by a lifetime of acceptance, listening, and prayer. Then, when the crises arise we
may be able to minister that intimate healing of which
Benedict speaks.

CHAPTER XLVII
ON INDICATING THE HOUR FOR THE WORK OF GOD

To give the signal for the Work of God, whether by day or by night, is the responsibility of the Abbot. He may do it himself or he may lay the charge on a brother sufficiently responsible to ensure that everything is performed at the correct time. The intoning of Psalms and antiphons is to be done in turn after the Abbot by those appointed. No one should venture to sing or read unless he can do it to the edification of his hearers. It is to be done with humility, gravity and reverence, and by appointment of the Abbot.

క్ష

Marching into church to sing the Office eight times a day is considered work by Benedict. The word 'liturgy' comes from two Greek words meaning 'people' and 'work' so it is not wrong to define 'liturgy' as 'the work of the people of God'. It is part of the monk's three-fold work along with divine reading and manual labour. These three types of work involve the whole person. The work of praising God involves the spirit, the work of divine reading strengthens the mind, while manual work involves the body. The three types of work function like a little trinity which helps to integrate the whole person.

In an age when everything, including worship, has to be entertaining we often forget that worshipping God is work that requires discipline and practise. If our children are

204

inclined to neglect worship because it is 'boring' it is our responsibility to remind them that, like anything worth doing, worship requires discipline and routine. The best way to do this is to institute a set time for family prayers and to stick to it. Of course we must make family prayers accessible and relevant for the children, but they don't have to be 'entertaining' as such. So Benedict emphasizes that the prayers are to be led with 'humility, gravity and reverence'.

So from the earliest age the children learn that worship is a fixed point – a duty which cannot be neglected. A routine time of family prayer also actively inculcates the understanding that worship is not the result of a sudden impulse or spontaneous whim. If the prayers are led with reverence they also learn the language of true worship. When a routine of family prayer is maintained the child learns, and we are also reminded, that worship is not an extra, but an essential. It is not like eating sweets. It is like cleaning our teeth.

Benedict places the responsibility for establishing a fixed time of worship firmly with the abbot. In our own homes fathers should be the prayer leaders. Do we have a set time and place for our own prayers? Do the rest of the family know that? At the end of the day our children will follow our example in life. They have no other chart to follow. So the *abba* of the family blazes the trail. If he does the others will find it a joy to follow.

CHAPTER XLVIII
ON DAILY MANUAL LABOUR (A)

Idleness is the enemy of the soul. For this reason the brethren should be occupied at certain times in manual labour, and at other times in sacred reading. Hence we think that the times for these two duties may be arranged as follows:

From Easter till 14 September, they should be set out in the morning and work at whatever is necessary from the first hour till about the fourth. from the fourth hour until about the sixth, they should be engaged in reading. After the sixth hour, and when they have had their meal, they may rest on their beds in complete silence, or if anyone has a mind to read, he may do so, but in such a way as not to disturb anyone else. None should be said rather early, at about the middle of the eighth hour, and then they should work again at whatever their tasks are until Vespers. If, however, local necessity or their own poverty compels them to work personally at gathering the harvest, they should not be upset about this. For then truly are they monks, if they live by the work of their hands, as did our Fathers and the Apostles. All their labours, however, should be kept under control on account of the less courageous.

❧

It is not easy to get children to join in the domestic chores. A lot of women might add, 'Neither is it easy to get husbands to join in the domestic chores'. The work of running a home is repetitious and tedious at best and dirty drudgery at worst. As in Benedict's time manual labour is the lowest social work and all of us want to avoid it.

But without being romantic about it, Benedict raises the status of manual labour to dignified human endeavour. When we get our hands dirty we are following the example of the first Egyptian monks who supported themselves with simple tasks. We are also following in the footsteps of the Apostles Peter and Paul, for Paul continued to earn his living as a tent-maker (1 Cor. 4.12; Acts 18.3), and early tradition records that Peter kept working as a fisherman during his travels to earn his keep.

Benedict realizes that there are many practical benefits of integrating manual work into our lives. Getting children involved in manual work becomes a school of values. They learn that no one is above a bit of manual work, and if they are paid for their domestic chores they soon learn the value of money. If they are made to follow through with routine tasks they learn how to maintain their lives automatically and cheerfully, and by finishing a domestic chore to the best of their ability they acquire new skills and learn how to finish a job once started.

But for Benedict there is more to manual labour than just the practical training in values. In the preceding section Benedict sees prayer as work; and here he sees work as prayer. So in the routine tasks at home our own manual work is to become a prayer. In mowing the lawn, sweeping the garage, mending an appliance or cooking a meal we should be serving others, and if prayer is at the heart of our lives, then the mundane and routine tasks will also have prayer at their heart. As such they will become incarnated prayers – actions of love and sacrifice for others.

This isn't easy, because we are inclined to treat tiresome domestic tasks as barriers to the 'real' activities which we would rather undertake. But if we can focus on even the smallest job with the attention that prayer fosters, then before long we will be learning to live more in the present moment, and that moment of life will become a fragment of prayer and surge with grace.

CHAPTER XLVIII
ON DAILY MANUAL LABOUR (B)

From 14 September until the beginning of Lent they should be free for reading till the end of the second hour. Then Terce should be said, and all should work at their allotted tasks until None. At the first signal for None every brother should detach himself from his work, so as to be ready for the sounding of the second signal. After their evening meal they should give themselves to reading or to studying the Psalms.

In Lent, however, the hours for reading are from the morning until the end of the third hour. Then until the end of the tenth hour they should work at their allotted tasks.

And during these days of Lent everyone should receive a book from the library, which he should read through from the beginning. These books are to be given out at the beginning of Lent. It is important that one or two seniors should be appointed to go round the monastery during the hours when the brethren are engaged in reading, to see whether perchance they come upon some lazy brother who is engaged in doing nothing or in chatter, and is not intent upon his book, and so not only profitless to himself but leading others astray. If such a one is found (which we hope will not be the case) he should be reprimanded once and a second time and if he does not amend, he should be punished in accordance with the Rule, so that the others may be warned.

Moreover, a brother should not be in the company of another at the wrong time.

❧

In this section on manual labour Benedict also deals with the third aspect of the monastic vocation: reading. In the Benedictine tradition this is not just reading for pleasure or education. Instead it is called *lectio divina*, divine reading. Just as Benedict considers prayer to be work and work prayer, so reading is also both work and prayer.

In an 'age of information' we are snowed under with a huge mass of verbiage. We are encouraged to learn 'speed-reading'. Furthermore, much of our reading is laid out in a way which encourages 'browsing', so we flit from article to article and from picture to picture searching for something which might just interest or entertain us for a moment. This short attention-span is encouraged by television which feeds our lust for entertainment at an ever more frenetic pace.

Lectio divina is something altogether different. In Benedict's day few could read, and those who could read had very few books to choose from. Therefore the activity of reading was like choosing diamonds from a jeweller's shop. Books were rare and precious, so divine reading meant reading slowly and meditatively, taking time to ponder, re-read and memorize the good bits. Divine reading is work, so it requires real effort. But it is also prayer, so it is an activity 'in-breathed' by the Holy Spirit.

Because the main book to be read was Holy Scripture, the same Spirit who inspired the writers and inspired the Church to select the canon also inspired the monastic copyists and those who read the Scripture. It should be the same today. Reading slowly allows time for the message to make the long journey from our head to our heart. Reading slowly and giving time for meditation allows the mind to ascend from meditation on the text to the prayer of contemplation.

These lessons can be applied practically in the home as we help our children learn to read. The beginning reader will naturally read slowly and out loud. So there is time to slow down to their pace, to help them discover words and compare meanings. Reading Bible stories during family prayers is an ideal time to practise *lectio divina*. The Bible stories should be told with care and time. Children may not be able to practise meditation with the stories, but they will be keen to act the stories out, discuss them and draw illustrations and create art projects about them. This an active way of meditating further on the Bible stories. Then as they are read, time should be taken to discuss them and draw out the deeper meanings. In this way the principle of *lectio divina* can live within the home, and the Word of God can be understood as a different book because it is treated specially. It becomes a special book because it is the book we pray with.

CHAPTER XLVIII
ON DAILY MANUAL LABOUR (C)

On Sunday all should give themselves to reading, except those to whom other duties have been assigned. But if anyone is so careless and idle that he is either unwilling or unable to study or read, he must be given some other task so as not to be unemployed.

To the brethren who are in poor health or not strong, the work or craft that is allotted should be such as to keep them occupied, but not such as by its weight to break them down or drive them away. Their lack of strength is a matter for the Abbot's consideration.

The Benedictine life seeks to balance the three activities: prayer, work and reading. Benedict treats all three as different forms of work. All three combine together to develop a whole person. Manual work keeps our feet on the ground. Prayer lifts our heart to heaven and reading opens our mind to Truth. But in today's chapter Benedict realizes that the Body of Christ is made up of many different members, and some monks will be better at one form of work than another. So the monk who finds reading a terrible chore is allowed to be engaged in some other useful task. The monk who is ill or weak can take on a lighter form of work.

So in our own communities some will spend more time

in intellectual labour, some will take up the domestic duties more. Others will be better at praying. Different things come naturally to different people. This is all the more reason why community is essential. We benefit from the strengths and interests of others. Benedict wants to establish a balance between the intellectual, the spiritual and the physical through his emphasis on reading, prayer and work. He wants this balance within each individual, but he also says that the full balance is only possible as we live in community. So the clever family member, the creative or sporty family member and the spiritual family member all encourage one another and balance the overall development.

An even fuller balance is to be found as the family relates to the wider world, for there what is lacking in our own family is fulfilled through others. There we find a wider perspective and a deeper appreciation of other people, other religions and other viewpoints. So the Christian family must never be insular. The nuclear community must be ever looking outside itself in service, in friendship and in real interaction with the community of the whole world. In constantly opening our family's awareness to the outside world we not only widen our education, but we come to affirm all of God's goodness and integrate it into our lives.

Benedict says the weakness of a particular monk is the concern of the abbot. So the *abba* in the family should see the big picture, being aware of one person's weakness and another person's strengths and weaving them together to bring the balance and harmony in the family community which reflects the unity of the Trinity itself.

CHAPTER XLIX
THE OBSERVANCE OF LENT

Although the monk's life ought at all seasons to bear a Lenten character such strength is found only in the few. Therefore we urge the brethren to keep the days of Lent with a special purity of life and also at this holy season to make reparation for the failings of other times. This reparation will be worthily performed if we guard ourselves from all our faults and apply ourselves to prayer with tears, to reading, to compunction of heart and to abstinence. Therefore at this season let us increase in some way the normal standard of our service, as for example, by special prayers, or by a diminution in food and drink; and so let each one spontaneously in the joy of the Holy Spirit make some offering to God concerning the allowance granted him. Thus he may reduce food and drink for his body, or his sleep, or his talkativeness or his looseness in speech, and so with the joy of spiritual desire, look forward to holy Easter.

But every brother should propose to the Abbot whatever he intends to offer, and it should be performed with his blessing and approval. For anything done without the permission of the spiritual father will be put down to presumption and vainglory, and deserving no reward. Everything, therefore, must be carried out with the approval of the Abbot.

❧

All Christians should be Lenten people. This means we are sojourners in a wilderness. Like the children of Israel who travelled forty years through the desert to the promised land, we travel through this life of 'forty days' to the eternal Easter of heaven. The significance of Lent gives this chapter its unique and wonderful tone of joy. Each one is to decide 'spontaneously in the joy of the Holy Spirit' what offering he will make to God.

For Benedict Lent is a season not only of self-denial, but also of taking on new responsibilities. The fasting is not an end in itself, but is there so that 'with the joy of spiritual desire [we will] look forward to holy Easter'. All this evokes the eagerness with which Benedict first encouraged us to 'run the path of God's commandments with an inexpressible delight of love'. In this passage more than any other Benedict hands over the spiritual decision to the individual. Each one is to choose the Lenten discipline which he wishes to undertake. This is a reminder that Lenten sacrifices, like all our spiritual duties, are meant to be undertaken willingly and with a sense of joy.

Maintaining a sense of joy in the Christian life is not easy. So often Christian groups try to manufacture joy and peace, but joy cannot be produced from grinning. Nor can it be manufactured with lots of cheerful songs and inspiring preaching. The result of such efforts is artificial. Instead Benedict very wisely points us to the source of real joy. Real, profound joy is linked with our ultimate share in Christ's resurrection. We experience that joy as we lay down our lives in service in order to run to our final destination in Christ. This is the joy of the long-distance runner – the joy which comes from stripping away everything and running for the goal with exhausting but exhilarating freedom (1 Cor. 9.25–27; Phil. 3.12–14).

Benedict's advice about Lent applies equally well in the home. Each child, as he gets old enough, should be encouraged to think of their own way of celebrating Lent. We should have suggestions of creative ways for them to make a sacrifice or take on some new service. As Benedict says, the emphasis should not be gloomy or hard. Instead, Lent should be seen as a joyful exercise, a time of training when the whole family runs together towards the celebration of Christ's victory.

CHAPTER L
BRETHREN WHO ARE FAR FROM THE ORATORY OR ON A JOURNEY

Brethren whose work is at a considerable distance, and who cannot reach the oratory at the right time – and the Abbot recognises this to be the case – should perform the Work of God in the place where they are working, kneeling down in deep respect to God. And likewise those who are travelling should not allow the hours prescribed for prayer to go unobserved, but they should do their best to carry out their duties in God's service and not neglect them.

❧

Benedict wants his monks to observe seven points of prayer during the day even if their work keeps them from the oratory, or they are away on a journey. He recognizes that those on a journey would not have had an accurate timepiece and so asks them to 'do their best' to keep the prayer points during the day.

In our fast-paced society we may find keeping our seven prayer points almost impossible. On the other hand, we all have watches and clocks, so to keep our appointments with God should be much easier. In chapter sixteen it was suggested that seven points of prayer might be: 1. on getting out of bed; 2. at breakfast; 3. at our mid-morning break; 4. at lunch; 5. at our mid-afternoon break; 6. at the evening meal; 7. at bedtime. These prayer points might simply consist of a brief prayer of blessing over the meal or a short time of reflection taken from a pocket-sized prayer book, Bible or devotional book. An excellent resource for such prayer is the Divine Office. The full version includes an Office of readings, morning prayer, midday prayer, evening prayer and a night Office. Shorter versions are available. Any of them might be suitable for our particular timetable and routine.

In all of this Benedict's exhortation to 'do our best' is both a challenge and a gentle reminder that we must not drive ourselves too hard. Prayer is to be integrated with our whole life, and our particular rule of life is to keep that wholeness as its end goal. Strict legalism shifts our attention from the final goal to the particular rule. All it does is increase guilt and lay more burdens on us. Benedict wants us to keep the end in sight (1 Cor. 9.24). This will encourage us and challenge us at the same time.

The Christian family must keep the same ideal. There is a delicate balance to be maintained between our religious duties and the demands of ordinary life. We must get our priorities right, but we mustn't be so demanding about little religious rules that we lose the wider perspective and the ultimate good. So family prayers are important, and maintaining our religious obligations is necessary, even when we are on holiday. But when circumstances demand it, the religious observations must sometimes give way to the demands of love and sacrifice. As Benedict says, 'we must do our best' and let God do the rest.

CHAPTER LI
BRETHREN WHO GO OUT ON SHORT ERRANDS

If a brother is sent out on some errand, and expects to return to the monastery the same day, he must not presume permission to eat outside the monastery, even if the invitation is a very pressing one, unless he has been so instructed by the Abbot. Anyone who does otherwise is to be excommunicated.

~

When a monk is outside the monastery he is never to accept a meal without prior permission from the abbot. This seems like a harsh rule. What can be the purpose of a monk not accepting hospitality outside the monastery? I think Benedict is trying to prevent nostalgia for 'what might have been'. It would be a very tough monk indeed who did not envy a married layman after an evening in a home with wife, hearth, children and plenty of good food and wine. He would probably come back to his cold and lonely cell feeling sorry for himself and inclined to grumble. So Benedict forbids outside meals without permission.

Once again, the underlying principle is vitally important for our spiritual state. Part of the Benedictine vow is to cultivate stability of life. This means being rooted in the particular place and community where God has put us. Nothing undermines stability more than the perpetual longing for 'what might have been'. This is a particularly seductive form of covetousness. When we covet in this way we don't covet anything particular of our neighbour's: we covet *everything* of our neighbours. We want to be in his place totally. But this longing for 'what might have been, is an illusion. We see in the other person's life all the good without seeing the underlying sacrifices which it requires. Longing for 'what might have been' is at least a waste of time. At worst it can cause us to leave everything on a constant but fruitless search for 'happiness'. No wonder Benedict steps down hard on a practice which might encourage the discontent and covetousness which would lead a monk to leave the monastery to chase an illusion.

As our children mature they need to learn how to deal with attractive alternative lives. Our society offers them a whole plethora of seductive but artificial role models. Adolescents need to 'discover' themselves properly, and this might mean trying on various personae. Without stamping on this process we must also help them assess the different options. We must also be wary of those activities which will lead to disastrous choices for the future. Benedict is strict about no meals outside the monastery because of where it might lead. So we might have to be strict with teenagers about outside activities they want to be involved with. The activity might seem harmless in itself, but we should help them ask where it might end up.

CHAPTER LII
THE ORATORY OF THE MONASTERY

The oratory should correspond to its name, and not be used for any other purpose, nor to store things. When the Work of God has been completed all are to go out noiselessly, and let reverence for God reign there. So that if a brother should have a mind to pray by himself, he will not be disturbed by the ill-conduct of anyone else. Moreover, also on other occasions, if someone wishes to make a private prayer, let him go in without hesitation and pray, not, however, aloud, but with tears, and the attention of his heart. Anyone therefore, who is not engaged on such a task, is not allowed to remain in the oratory after the Work of God, as we said above, lest someone else be disturbed.

In setting down physical instructions for the oratory or chapel, Benedict also gives us instruction on prayer. The oratory should be a silent place set aside totally for prayer. It is not to be cluttered up as a store-room, but should be filled only with the 'reverence for God'. So too our prayer lives should not be cluttered up with long, loud prayers. Instead we should pray in attentive silence. This is the heart of monastic prayer – our whole being turned to God in fervent love, or, as Benedict puts it in chapter twenty, in 'pure devotion'. So our hearts, like the oratory, should be the place where the reverence for God reigns.

In chapter forty-seven Benedict makes it clear that there

should be set times for prayer. Here he makes sure there is also a fixed place. So in our homes, if there is room, it is a good idea to set aside a *poustinia*, a Russian word for hermitage. The little hermitage is a quiet place within the home or garden. Decorated simply with a focus such as an icon, or a candle, it can be that 'secret room' for prayer of which our Lord speaks (Matt. 6.6). If a whole room cannot be given over, then a corner of a room. In even the smallest home a mantelpiece can be transformed into an altar with the addition of candles and an icon. Setting up the prayer place and lighting the candles is an activity for the younger children to enjoy.

Because of our physical nature we are bound by time and place. Some prayer techniques lead us to think escape from time and place are beneficial. This is alien to Benedict's thought and alien to the heart of Christianity. Benedict has a perspective on time and place which is fully incarnational. Because he establishes set times and places for prayer he does not seek to escape the constraints of time and place: rather, he enters into the constraints and redeems them from the inside out. This is always the action of incarnation – to redeem the limitation or the sin from within.

Finally, as Catherine de Hueck Doherty points out, the *poustinia* or sacred space must ultimately be located within our hearts and minds. We must carry within us an 'oratory of the heart', an uncluttered place of stillness and peace which has been constructed and maintained by prayer.

CHAPTER LIII
THE RECEPTION OF GUESTS (A)

All who arrive as guests are to be welcomed like Christ, for he is going to say, 'I was a stranger and you welcomed me.' The respect due to their station is to be shown to all, particularly to those of one family with us in the faith and to pilgrims. As soon as a guest is announced he should be met by the superior or by brethren with every expression of charity, and first of all they should pray together, and then greet one another with the kiss of peace. This kiss of peace should not be offered until after prayer has been said, since the devil sometimes plays tricks. When guests arrive or depart the greatest humility should be shown in addressing them: so, let Christ who is received in them be adored with bowed head or prostrate body.

So when the guests have been welcomed they should be led to prayer, and then either the superior or someone delegated by him should sit with them. The Divine Law should be read to them for their edification, and after this every kindness should be shown to them. The superior may break the fast for the sake of a guest unless it happens to be an important fast day which cannot be waived; the brethren, however, should keep their accustomed fasts.

*The Abbot should give all the guests water to wash their hands, and with the whole community he should wash their feet. When they have done so, they should recite the verse, **We have received your mercy, O God, in the midst of your temple**.*

Special care is to be shown in the reception of the poor and of pilgrims, for in them especially is Christ received; for the awe felt for the wealthy imposes respect enough of itself.

☙

Here in one of his most famous maxims Benedict says guests should be welcomed like Christ. This is a reminder that Christ judges our treatment of strangers as a reflection of our love for him (Matt. 25.35). Benedict doesn't mention it, but Hebrews 13.1 is also an excellent reference. There the writer to the Hebrews says, 'always remember to welcome strangers, for by doing this, some have entertained angels without knowing it.' The verse points to two Scriptural stories: Abraham entertaining the three strangers at the oaks of Mamre (Genesis 18), and Christ appearing as a stranger on the road to Emmaus (Luke 24). Furthermore, in exercising hospitality, the abbot and the cellarer exhibit the characteristics of the church elders as set down by St Paul in 1 Timothy 3 and Titus 1, for in both passages he says the elder must be hospitable.

This chapter on hospitality is well situated shortly after the rule forbidding monks to stay for meals outside the monastery. The prohibition on enjoying hospitality outside the monastery is balanced by the injunction to offer the warmest hospitality to guests who come to them. Benedictines are well known for observing this part of the rule faithfully. For many reasons visitors are important to the enclosed monks. Through visitors they stay in touch with the outside world. Through hospitality they minister Christ's love to the needy. Hospitality is also a form of evangelism, for through a warm welcome the monks show the love of Christ to others. Furthermore, the guests join in with the reading and prayer of the community and so begin to taste that love which inspires its spiritual life.

Hospitality is greatly overlooked in our self-sufficient age. Too often we lead oyster lives, enclosed in our comfortable little shells. But opening the doors of our home to others is an excellent way to share Christ's love. Hospitality is an expression of vulnerability and openness.

As a method of caring for others it is natural and intimate. We cannot hold the needy at a distance once they've entered our home, so genuine hospitality is an expression of the whole Christian life (1 Pet. 4.9–10). Finally, by having an open door our children accept that we share all things both within the home and with those who are outside, for they too are our mothers and fathers and brothers and sisters. They too are to be welcomed as Christ.

CHAPTER LIII
THE RECEPTION OF GUESTS (B)

The kitchen for the Abbot and guests should be separate, so that when guests arrive at unforeseeable times (and they are always coming to a monastery) they may not disturb the brethren. Two brethren capable of performing this duty should take over this kitchen for a year. Help should be given them as they need it, so that they may serve without complaining, and also, when they have less work to do, they should leave their kitchen to work wherever they are bidden. And this principle applies not only to them but to all departments of the monastery: help is to be provided for those in need, and when they have spare time, they must obey their orders.

Also, with regard to the guests' quarters, a brother should be put in charge, whose soul is filled with the fear of God. A sufficient number of beds should be kept ready there. And let God's house be wisely cared for by wise men.

No one without specific instructions is to associate or converse with the guests. If a brother should meet or see one, he should, as we have said, give him a humble greeting, and then ask a blessing and go on his way, explaining that he is not allowed to converse with a guest.

❧

Benedict wants the monastic community to welcome guests with all the warmth possible, but he also realizes that the monastery is not a hotel, hostel or hospital. So in today's reading he establishes some boundaries. There is to be a separate kitchen and guesthouse for the guests so they can be received without disturbing the brethren. A guest master is appointed to look after the guests' accommodation. He is to be a man 'filled with the fear of God', one who will not be tempted to establish too close a relationship with guests. Finally, Benedict says the ordinary monk is not to converse with guests.

This seems to run counter to the warm welcome which the community is meant to offer. But Benedict realizes that guests are not to distract the community from their primary vocation, and that if the monks spend all the time with guests they will in the end have nothing unique to offer the guests. It is only by establishing boundaries and preserving the monastic life that the monastery can offer its unique life to its many visitors.

We have the same tension in the Church. On the one hand, we want the Church to be a place of welcome and refuge for all people. It should be the great tree which provides a nesting-place for every sort of bird (Matt. 13.32). But unless we defend the faith and set up boundaries, the faith we wish to share will be eroded.

Likewise, in the home we walk a tightrope in regard to outside influences. We are commanded to be 'in the world, but not of the world' (Rom. 12.2). So we must constantly weigh up the 'visitors' to our religious community, the family. Benedict wanted to preserve the monastic life and protect the monks from too much 'worldly' influence. In the same way we should always be monitoring the influences our children receive through television, magazines and the media. What sort of 'guests' are we allowing into the minds and souls of our children? We should also help our children choose good friends from the earliest age. This is not to encourage snobbery, but simply to help them see how good friendships build up while bad friends corrupt and destroy. So we must welcome outward influences on the family, but we must also be careful to protect the souls put in our charge.

CHAPTER LIV
WHETHER A MONK SHOULD RECEIVE LETTERS OR OTHER GIFTS

On no account may a monk, without the Abbot's permission, either accept (or give) letters or offerings of blessed bread or small gifts of any kind whether from his parents or other people or his brethren. And if something is sent to him, even from his parents, he must not take upon himself to accept it before it has been shown to the Abbot. If the Abbot allows it to be accepted, it rests with him to decide to whom it shall be given, and the brother to whom it was sent must not be upset, so that no opportunity is given the evil one. If anyone should be headstrong enough to act otherwise he must submit to the discipline of the Rule.

~

Here Benedict reasserts his prohibition against personal possessions. But in this chapter he reveals a different motive. In this section he deals with the monks' attitude to the outside world. They are not to stay for a meal outside the monastery lest they become discontented. They are to welcome guests, but Benedict advises caution lest the visitors disturb the monastic life. Here he forbids the receipt of gifts and letters. I think he does so not only to eliminate private property, but also to help the monks break free from outside connections to family and friends.

In his commitment to the monastery the monk follows the gospel commandment to give up even mother and father for the sake of the Kingdom (Matt. 10.37–39). So the monk forsakes his natural family for the family of the monastery, the family of God. Detachment from potentially destructive outside forces is one thing; this detachment from family love is a harder principle to embrace. And yet it is a recurrent theme through the gospel. We naturally place our family commitments among the highest in our lives. But Christ says they are not the ultimate priority.

This truth applies to all our familial relationships. If we want God's love we must be able to let go our lesser loves. This doesn't mean we reject our wives or children; instead we realize that we cannot love them in a way that excludes God. God's love must be brought into the heart of our family love. A three-way relationship then develops and God's love becomes the bond which unites us most deeply. When two people place their ultimate focus on God their own relationship becomes intertwined and empowered with God's love. So St John says that 'those who live in love live in God and God lives in them' (1 John 4.16). When this three-way love develops in a marriage and within the home the divine family of the Holy Trinity becomes a living reality within our own homes.

So Benedict's prohibition on gifts and letters from family is an attempt to break the monk's affection for the outside world – even his friends and family – so that he can be wedded more completely to God. This hard ruling reminds us that our good human loves may be the enemy of the best divine love, and that if we do not weave God's higher love into our lesser loves we may end up losing both.

CHAPTER LV
THE CLOTHING AND FOOTWEAR OF THE BRETHREN (A)

Clothing should be given to the brethren according to the nature of the district where they live and the climate, because in cold places more is needed and in warm ones less. This is for the Abbot to consider. It is our view that in temperate localities, it will be sufficient for monks if each has a cowl and a tunic – the cowl should be woolly in winter, but thin or worn in summer – and a scapular for work. For footwear he should have stockings and shoes. The monks should not argue about the colour or coarseness of all these things, but accept what is available in the region where they live or can be bought cheaply.

But the Abbot should take care about the size of these clothes, that they are not too short for those who use them, but of the right size. Those who receive new clothes should always give the old ones back at once; they can be stored in the wardrobe for the benefit of the poor. For it is sufficient for a monk to have two tunics and two cowls, to allow for wear at night and for washing: more than that is superfluous, and should be taken away. Their stockings also and anything that is old should be returned by them when they get new ones.

Those who are sent on a journey should get drawers from the wardrobe, which they should wash and give back on their return. And their cowls and tunics should be in rather better condition than those they usually have; they should get them from the

230

*wardrobe when they set out on this journey, and give them back
on their return.*

∞

All through the Rule Benedict integrates a concern for
physical things with the spiritual and emotional welfare of
his monks. In this chapter he takes precise care over the
treatment of clothes. In seeking to avoid vanity and
useless luxury it might be easy for the spiritual person to
disregard his appearance and wear any old clothes that
are to hand. But Benedict avoids such carelessness. He
realizes that our outward dress indicates our inward attitude. So his usual moderation and generosity of spirit is
exercised. Clothing is to be well-fitting, clean and cared for
with a methodical and gentle reverence.

He wants the clothes to be warm and hard-wearing, but
practicality is not his only aim; care is to be taken that the
clothes fit well, and that the monk is kitted out more
smartly when he is on a journey. Research shows that we
all work better and feel better when we take the trouble to
dress neatly. Dressing well shows that we have a proper
respect and love for ourselves and the wonderful bodies
God has given us. So we should have a proper delight in
good clothes of an appropriate style. At the same time we
should have a healthy disregard for clothes that are poor
quality or reflect some shallow, sexy or stupid fashion.

We'll take similar care with our children's clothing.
Every child loves getting new clothes and shoes. There's
nothing wrong with wearing 'hand-me-downs' – Benedict's monks share their clothes – but we should also make
an effort to buy new clothes for each child to take pride in.
Our concern to dress the children well is a small but
important indication of our care for them. If a child
becomes obsessed with a particular fashion item it is not a
bad idea for them to save up the money to buy it. Before
long they'll realize what poor value high-priced fashion
items represent.

Finally, clothes are important to Benedict because they
reflect the inner state. 'The cowl does not make the monk',

but clothes that are simple, dignified and practical show an individual who has established balance and taste. Thomas Traherne said, 'All things are yours and you were made to prize them according to their value.' So clothes are there for warmth, modesty, and to help us look good and feel good. If we use them to preen and strut or establish status we prize them in the wrong way and remain blind to their true value.

CHAPTER LV
THE CLOTHING AND FOOTWEAR OF THE BRETHREN (B)

For bedding, a mattress, a blanket, a coverlet and a pillow are enough. The beds should be frequently inspected by the Abbot as a precaution against private possessions. If anyone is found to have anything which was not given him by the Abbot, he is to undergo the severest punishment; and that this vice of personal ownership may be totally eliminated, everything necessary should be given by the Abbot; namely, a cowl, a tunic, stockings, shoes, a belt, a knife, a pen, a needle, a handkerchief and writing tablets, so that all excuses about necessity are removed. But the Abbot must always bear in mind the statement in the Acts of the Apostles that 'distribution was made to each according to his need.'

And so he must bear in mind the weakness of those in need, but not the ill-will of the envious. Indeed in all his decisions he must consider that God will repay.

❧

Again Benedict seeks to root out the weed of private ownership. The monks are given precisely what they need and no more. This section reminds us of Benedict's military analogy in the Prologue. The monk is a soldier, and here his lean list of belongings sounds like the necessary items doled out to each soldier on the first day of his basic training. The practical poverty of the monks is also a sharp reminder that Benedict wrote for men who lived in a society which was comparatively poor. What they had in terms of food, clothing and possessions was similar to what their peasant neighbours had.

We may not prohibit private ownership to the extent that Benedict does, but it does us no harm to examine our attitude to wealth. Do we really need to strive for more and more and bigger and bigger? And with that increasing wealth do we really want to 'move up' into an ever-dazzling social circle? Benedict seems to be asking his monks not 'how much can you acquire?' but 'how little do you require?' In his chapter on humility Benedict advises going down, not going up. Humility and wealth rarely live together.

Making a deliberate choice to scale down our life-style is dangerous and radical. But it can bring enormous freedoms we never knew were possible. When we analyse our career perhaps we should not necessarily look for promotion, but instead discover how we can find a less demanding job which gives us more time with the family, even if it means a cut in pay. If both mother and father work, is it to obtain necessities or luxuries? If the latter, why bother? It is worth the stress? Asking 'how little can we live on?' rather than 'how much can we get?' will eventually transform our attitude to everything.

An attitude of simplicity in the home is also a great gift to our children. The child who has learned to get by on a little will always be able to cope with having a lot, whereas the child who has had everything will think any loss a terrible deprivation. Those who have just what they need can learn inner contentment but those who always have everything will never have enough.

CHAPTER LVI
THE ABBOT'S TABLE

The Abbot should always take his meals with the guests and pilgrims. Whenever there are no guests he may at his own discretion invite to his table from among the brethren those whom he wishes, but one or two seniors should always be left with the brethren for the sake of discipline.

The abbot maintains his own 'high table' for guests, and when there are no guests he invites certain of the brothers to join him. This detail not only shows that Benedict expected there to be a steady flow of guests to the monastery, but also that the abbot was the chief host. However, this hierarchy of manners points to another picture. The abbot maintaining a 'high table' evokes the parable of the wedding feast. A guest takes the lower place and the host invites him to 'come up higher' (Luke 14.10). The monastic refectory then becomes an icon of the marriage feast of the Lamb pictured in the Book of Revelation with the abbot presiding as icon of Christ.

The picture also recalls George Herbert's poem, 'Love', in which the faithful soul sees his sin and only wishes to serve his Lord in simple gratitude, but the Lord beckons him to communion and fellowship. 'You must sit down, says Love, and taste my meat ...' and the soul finally yields: '... So I did sit and eat'. This wedding feast then points us to the Last Supper where Christ presides as host and invites us to share in the bread and wine which is his

Body and Blood. So Benedict establishes within the manners of the monastery a living icon which points to truths beyond the physical. This is a constant theme throughout the Rule. A mystical reading penetrates the physical details to see the spiritual significance, and as the spiritual significance is unlocked we begin seeing the whole world with 'sacramental eyes'.

This is not simply a contemplative insight. It inspires and motivates all of our Christian action as well. So as the hospitality of the Benedictine abbot pictures Christ inviting us to 'come up higher' at the wedding feast, so in chapter fifty-three we are told that every guest is to be received as Christ. Both are true. As Christ is both priest and victim in the eucharistic feast, so he is also guest and host. He welcomes us to the royal banquet, but he is also there in the most humble guest. Benedict would wish this 'way of seeing' to enlighten every aspect of our lives so that every bit of work, prayer and reading becomes imbued with the abiding light of Christ. This is the way toward constant prayer – the way towards our own transformation into the image and likeness of Christ himself.

CHAPTER LVII
THE CRAFTSMEN OF THE MONASTERY

If there are craftsmen in the monastery let them carry on their crafts in all humility, subject to the approval of the Abbot. But if any one of them becomes conceited because of his knowledge of his craft, which is apparently bringing profit to the monastery, he is to be taken away from his craft; nor is he to come back to it, unless, after he has shown humility, the Abbot gives him a new permission. If anything produced by the craftsmen is to be sold, those responsible for the transaction must take care not to venture to do anything fraudulent. They should always keep in mind the fate of Ananias and Sapphira, lest the death which those persons incurred in the body, they (and any who practise fraud in the affairs of the monastery) should themselves undergo in their souls.

With regard to the prices charged, the sin of avarice must not creep in; but whatever is sold should be a little cheaper than is possible for lay-persons, 'so that God may be glorified in all things.'

✿

In the secular world the need to make money provides a powerful motivation for hard work and excellence. If we don't provide a first-rate service or product someone else will. Competition is exciting. It presents a challenge and gives our working life a driving force. Benedict allows for a measure of competition, but doesn't permit any hint of a proud spirit. The monk who has a particular skill is to exercise it with the abbot's oversight for the good of the whole community. The summary of the whole matter is in Benedict's final quotation from 1 Peter 4.11 – 'so that God may be glorified in all things'.

This quotation sums up the Benedictine way. Every thought, word and action is aimed toward this higher goal – the glory of God. This is not easy when our daily work takes place in a rabidly competitive market-place. How can we do everything to the glory of God when we have to be fiercely competitive to do our job? Benedict hints at a clever solution when he says prices should be lower than is possible for the competition. Why were the monks able to offer lower prices? Because their simple lifestyle meant their overheads were lower. So if we run our businesses along simple lines, focusing on quality provision for basic needs, we will be competitive naturally and properly. In other words competitive prices and practices are perfectly valid. What matters is the motivation.

Bringing this deeper motivation into our place of business is an important witness. If we really live a simple life, working hard for higher goals, our colleagues will soon catch the spirit. At heart most people want to work for more than just money and our set of values may open up new ways of seeing for those who wish to grow.

Finally, this chapter points the way for our children to deal properly with their talents. It is our sacred role to help them discover and develop their natural giftedness. In doing this we must also help them to see that the gift is from God. It is their duty and joy to develop the gift, but it is also their duty and joy to give God the glory for all their accomplishments. This does not mean a grim surrender, but a joyful acknowledgement that their own success is the blossoming of God's infilling, creative power.

CHAPTER LVIII
THE RULES FOR RECEIVING BRETHREN (A)

Easy admission is not to be granted to anyone as soon as he applies to enter the monastic state, but as the Apostle says, 'Test the spirits to see whether they are of God.' But if the newcomer continues to knock on the door, and it is seen that he puts up patiently with the unkind replies and the difficulty of getting in, and that after four or five days he is still persisting in his request, then let him be allowed to come in, and remain in the guest quarters for a few days. After that he should be in the quarters of the novices, where they work and eat and sleep. And to them should be assigned a senior monk who has the gift of winning souls, and he should pay them the closest attention. His care must be to find out whether the newcomer sincerely seeks God, whether he is earnest at the Work of God, in obedience and under severe words. All the things that are hard and repugnant to nature in the way to God are to be expounded to him.

If he promises to persevere in his intention to remain, after two months have passed, this Rule is to be read to him from beginning to end, and he is to be told, 'This is the law under which you are asking to live. If you can keep it, come in; if, however, you cannot, freely depart.' If he still stands his ground, then he is to be led to the above-mentioned novices' quarter, and once again his patience under all kinds of trials is to be put to the test. After the passing of another six months, the Rule is to be read to him so that he may know what he is entering on. If he still remains, after four months the same Rule is to be read to him again. Then, if, having thought the matter over carefully, he promises to keep all the rules, and to obey all the orders given him, he should be admitted into the community. He must, however, realise that it is set down in the law of the Rule that from that day onward he may not leave the monastery, nor cast off from his neck the yoke of the Rule which it was open to him during all this lengthy deliberation to decline or to undertake.

Benedict makes it difficult to enter the monastery. From the beginning the man wishing to become a monk is rejected. Once he is admitted as a notice he goes through a period of testing during which he is assessed by the novice master. So he won't take it lightly, the Rule is read to him three times in twelve months. The whole twelve-month period is like a spiritual boot camp. Only the tough recruits will survive and make it to 'officer status'.

Too often we are tempted to look at choices in life romantically. Just as it is easy to view marriage through heart-shaped, rose-tinted spectacles, so it is easy to view the monastic life romantically. Either it looks like an easy option or it appeals as a secure escape route from the demands of real life. Maybe we are drawn by the medievalism of it or a romantic notion of the simplicity and holiness of the life. Benedict has no time for such sugar-frosting, and his initial time of testing is designed to knock any such view of the spiritual life firmly on the head.

We do well to consider his approach in our own attitude to the spiritual life. Are we seriously seeking God, or are we attracted to a spiritual never-never land where we won't have to grow up? If we were more realistic to start with we wouldn't be quite so disappointed when the path of perfection turns out to be full of trials and hardship. Benedict makes the point from the beginning that we are soldiers of Christ or athletes training to run in the path of God's commandments. So he establishes a heavy dose of realism for anyone who aspires to such a life.

It is not easy to give our children a realistic appraisal of life. We naturally want to shield them from life's harsh realities, but we only spoil them if we do. So from an early age there should be an element in our life together which looks for challenges and works hard to overcome them. Even if it is the discipline of keeping a room tidy or practising a musical instrument, the principle is set down that hard work and grit is needed to succeed. This lesson will serve them in good stead in every area of life, but especially in their spiritual progress.

CHAPTER LVIII
THE RULES FOR RECEIVING BRETHREN (B)

The one who is to be accepted into the community must promise in the oratory, in the presence of all, stability, conversion of life and obedience. He is to do this before God and all his saints, so that if he subsequently behaves otherwise, he will know that he merits condemnation by him the one whom he mocks. With regard to this promise he must write a petition, calling on the names of the saints whose relics are there, and in the name of the Abbot who is present. This petition he should write with his own hand or, if he is illiterate, it must be written by another whom he has asked, and the novice must make his sign on it. And he should place it with his own hand on the altar. When he has done so, the novice himself straight away intones this verse, **Accept me, Lord, according to your word, and I shall live, and you will not disappoint me in my hope.** *The whole community repeats this verse three times, adding* **Glory be to the Father** *at the end. Then the brother novice prostrates himself at the feet of each of the brethren, asking their prayers. Then from that day onwards he is to be reckoned among the community. If he has any possessions, he must either previously give them to the poor, or by means of a formal donation give them to the monastery, keeping for himself nothing at all, since he realises that from that day he will have no power even over his own body. At once then in the oratory, let him be stripped of his own clothes which he is wearing, and reclothed in those of the monastery. The clothes,* *however, which have been taken from him must be placed in the wardrobe, and kept there, so that if at some later time he should agree to the suggestion of the devil that he should leave the monastery (which God forbid), he can be stripped of the clothing of the monastery, befcre being sent away. He does not, however, get back the petition which the Abbot took off the altar, but it is kept in the monastery.*

☙

Once he has gone through a year's induction the novice may take his solemn vows. Nowadays the period of the novitiate is extended, and customs vary among different Benedictine communities as to how long a monk or nun is trained before solemn vows. But despite the changes, the solemn vow is still the turning-point of the monastic life. There the Benedictine promises before God and his brothers to follow the way of stability, conversion of life and obedience. He is then committed for life and receives the final part of his monastic habit.

We took our solemn vows when we were married. Like the monk, we entered into a lifelong relationship with a religious community – our Christian family. Like the monk, we chose certain aspects of that community, but had to take others on trust. So we chose a wife, but not our in-laws or our children. As the monk must accept every member of the community, so we have to learn to love those we are given.

The monk promises stability, conversion of life and obedience. We have spoken of these in more detail in the introduction, but it is good to be reminded that within the demands of Christian marriage we too must strive for stability, conversion of life and obedience. Stability is a state of mind which accepts that everything necessary can be learned where we are. As one Desert Father put it: 'Stay in your cell and your cell will teach you everything.' Conversion of life means no less than a total transformation of our whole being into the likeness of Christ. This does not simply mean changing our habits, but allowing ourselves to be changed from the inside out. Marriage and family life provide the crucible for this transforming fire. And in constant self-sacrificial service to our wives and children we discover the heart of obedience.

This is not to equate the married and the monastic vocation in an easy comparison; but neither the monastic nor the married vocation is superior. A good Christian husband and father may have run further on the path than a negligent monk and vice versa. When taken with proper seriousness both vocations are equal, but different. Each sheds light on the other. Each reveals to the other a profound way of living in love and running on the path of God's commandments.

CHAPTER LIX
THE SONS OF THE RICH OR THE POOR WHO ARE OFFERED

If it happens that a nobleman offers his son to God as a monk, and the child is still of tender age, the parents should make out the petition of which we have spoken. They should wrap this petition and the boy's hand together with the Mass offering in the altar cloth and offer him in that way. As for their property, they must in the same petition promise under oath that on no occasion will they ever give him anything either themselves or through an agent or by any other means, nor will they afford him any opportunity for possessing anything. However, if they are unwilling to do this, and want to have the merit of giving something as an alms to the monastery, they should make a donation to the monastery of whatever they want to give; they may reserve the income of it to themselves if they wish. Thus will be blocked every way by which expectation might remain to deceive the child and (God forbid), lead him to destruction, as we have learnt by experience.

And poorer people may follow the same procedure. As for those who possess nothing at all, they may simply make the petition and offer their son with the Mass offering in the presence of witnesses.

⌘

An oblate was originally a boy who was offered to the monastery by his parents. If the parents could afford it they also offered a portion of land or a significant gift to the monastery, ostensibly for the upkeep of the child. In the thirteenth century the noble family of St Thomas Aquinas offered him as an oblate to the great abbey of Monte Cassino.

When parents gave one of their sons to be a monk they were doing what they considered best for everyone involved. In practical terms the boy would receive a good education, have a secure future and the chance to live a rewarding and sacrificial life. The family would benefit from the prayers of their son and his whole community. The wider society also benefited, as sons filled the ranks of the monastic system which served the whole wider community. Nevertheless, the idea that we should 'give' our child to a monastery now appals us. But is it so alien to the way we treat our children anyway?

When parents gave their sons to the monastery in the Middle Ages they yielded their child to the institution which epitomized the beliefs and values of the whole society. When we send our children to boarding-school, or insist that they perform well at school 'in order to get a good job', aren't we just as effectively 'giving them' to the system of the day? The main difference is that giving a child to the monastery was a way of giving him to God. When we 'give a child' to the system of the day we are usually sacrificing him or her to Mammon.

The underlying principle of the oblate is of course that of oblation or sacrifice. In a deeper way when we bring our children for baptism we are offering them to God, and we must always keep in the forefront of our minds that our children are lent to us by God. He has entrusted them to us. Our job is to give them back to him daily, and as the medieval parent made the oblation with a gift, so we must offer our children to God with the gift of our own lives. As the medieval oblate was trained for God's service in the monastery, so we must train and instruct our children – not for ourselves, but for the greater glory of God. In this respect each one of our children should be oblates. If we don't physically give them to monasteries any more, our yielding them to God should be no less total.

CHAPTER LX
PRIESTS WHO MAY WANT TO LIVE IN THE MONASTERY

If anyone of the rank of priest asks to be taken into the monastery, this should not be granted him too quickly. If, however, he is very persistent in his request, he must understand that he will have to observe the full discipline of the Rule and that no relaxation will be made for him, as the Scripture says, 'Friend, for what purpose have you come?' Nevertheless it may be granted him to stand next to the Abbot, to pronounce blessings, and to celebrate Mass, provided the Abbot gives permission. Otherwise he must not take any privilege for granted, knowing that he is subject to the discipline of the Rule, and should give greater proofs of humility to all. Moreover, in the event of some appointment or other monastic business coming up for consideration, he must keep the position in the community which goes with the date of his entry into the monastery, and not the one granted him out of reverence for the priesthood.

If any clerics should show the same desire to join the monastery, they should be placed in a slightly advanced position in the community, and they, too, must promise observance of the Rule and stability.

❧

It should always be remembered that Benedict was a layman, and his Rule establishes guidelines for a community of laymen. As such the monastic house functions in a unique way within the hierarchy of the Church. The abbot has the rank of a bishop so the monastery is almost like a church within a Church. So Benedict is careful about admitting priests to the monastery because they have worked within a different authority-structure and may expect the same rules within the monastery. Benedict places them amongst all the other monks. Their priestly role can be exercised, but it is just one among many gifts in the monastic community.

This chapter offers excellent direction for the Church today. Too often priests bear a heavy burden in the parish. They wield all the power, but they also do all the work. Too many parishes and dioceses have yet to learn how the whole Church functions together as the body of Christ. Priests and bishops are very important in the body. If Christ is the head of the body, they might be likened to the hands and fingers. But as St Paul teaches, no part of the body must think it is sufficient on its own: we all need one another (1 Cor. 12.14–27).

However, the bishops and priests cannot delegate work and responsibility to the laity if we are not willing to shoulder our share. We may think the priest is 'on a pedestal', but too often it is the laity who put him there and keep him elevated because, quite frankly, he is safer up there out of the way like some plaster saint. This won't do. Benedict's vision of a priest fully integrated as part of the whole praying and working community is a model which can apply to each diocese and parish.

Benedict's principle of equality applies in the family as well. As the priest might feel he should have priority in the monastery, so each child may feel a 'right' to preferential treatment, either because they are oldest or youngest, or because they have special needs. Benedict wants them all to 'keep their position in the community' or 'stand in line' with all the others. It is up to the *abba*, with the mother, to recognize the needs of each one and minister to those individual needs with complete attention and love.

CHAPTER LXI
HOW TRAVELLING MONKS ARE TO BE RECEIVED (A)

If a travelling monk should arrive from some far-off locality, and want to live as a guest in the monastery, and be content with the customs that he finds there, and not disturb the community by making special demands, but be quite content with what he finds, then let him be accepted for as long as he desires. And if indeed with humble charity he reasonably criticises or points some things out, the Abbot should consider the matter carefully. For it may be that the Lord has sent him for this very purpose. And if later on he wants to settle down permanently, this desire is not to be refused, especially as his way of life could be well known during his time as a guest.

An outside monk makes a very different kind of visitor from the usual guests to a monastery. He comes in with his own knowledge of the monastic way and his own set of expectations, customs and habits. Benedict gives him a warm, but cautious welcome. If the visiting monk humbly accepts what he finds in the monastery then he may stay. Benedict also welcomes his comments and criticisms because an outside observer will often be able to see things which the members of the community, including the abbot, are blind to.

This attitude to outsiders is vital for our own individual life and family life. It is natural to put up barriers and construct a cosy enclave for ourselves within our home, parish and circle of friends. But Benedict wants us to have an open door of hospitality and an open mind towards new ideas. We should ask how much we really listen to others. Do we see their ideas and attitudes as fresh alternatives or as dangerous innovations? Do we take criticism as a creative challenge or a hostile threat? Do we have the deadly attitude: We've never done it that way before'? or do we accept new ideas with curiosity and enthusiasm?

If we cultivate an open-minded attitude it will pay dividends in our working life and in the home. With an open mind and heart we will always be on the look-out for fresh alternatives and creative ways of solving problems. Rather than assuming we know everything about everything, we will value the knowledge and insight of others in a whole range of disciplines.

Such open-mindedness lays a good foundation for our children's education. They have a natural curiosity and inquisitiveness which should be encouraged with lots of stimulus from outside the home. While we need to monitor what materials they read and watch we should also have a liberal attitude, allowing most things to be tasted, and explaining why some are right and others wrong. Benedict says outside opinion should be 'considered carefully'. He doesn't reject it outright. Neither does he accept everything without discrimination. The same should be true in our relationship to outside influences in our lives and in our homes.

CHAPTER LXI
HOW TRAVELLING MONKS ARE TO BE RECEIVED (B)

If on the other hand during that time, he should be found demanding or a man of bad habits, not only should he not be allowed to join the community but he should be frankly told to go away, for fear that others should be corrupted by his unhappy condition.

If, however, he is not the kind which deserves dismissal, not only should he be admitted to the community if he so petitions, but he should be persuaded to stay so that others may be instructed by his example, and because it is the one Lord we serve in every place, and the one King for whom the battle is fought. Indeed if the Abbot sees him to be of sufficient virtue, he may place him in a somewhat higher position. In fact the Abbot may assign a more honourable position than that due to the day of entry not only to a monk, but to one coming from the above-mentioned ranks of priests or clerics, if he recognises that their way of life is worthy of such treatment. The Abbot, however, must take care never to accept permanently a monk from another known monastery without either the agreement of his Abbot or a letter or recommendation, since it is written, 'Do not to another what you would not want done to yourself.'

❧

If the visiting monk proves to be a good recruit he should not only be welcomed, but actively encouraged to stay. Furthermore, if he can fill a valuable place in the community Benedict wants him to be given a position of leadership. The same applies to priests and clerics who, after a time of testing, prove able to take on greater responsibilities. So Benedict balances the natural wish for seniority with the common-sense placement of skilled personnel. The underlying principle is to maintain a delicate counterpoise between the proper respect due to elders and the recognition of gifted newcomers.

The same balance is necessary in business and family life. Certain people have pride of place due to seniority. Others establish their higher place by their own giftedness or hard work. Both must work in relationship with each other and not see the other party as a threat. In the workplace we must recognize the importance of experience and accumulated knowledge just as we must value the fresh ideas and up-to-date training of the new recruit. Within the family, grandparents should be a source of wisdom and insight, while the young are valued for their energy, innocence and enthusiasm. The old are enlivened by the young, while the young are instructed by the old.

A similar tension may develop between siblings. The oldest rightly takes a senior role in the family, but he may lack the confidence and zest which a younger child shows. The story of the prodigal son shows just such a relationship. The staid and faithful older brother lacks the *joie de vivre* and attractive rebelliousness of the younger brother. The father's reaction to both shows the good *abba's* response. The younger brother is always welcomed back and given a celebration feast. The older brother is valued because he is 'always there' with the father. So our relationship with different children will always include a nuanced interrelationship between the children themselves. As Benedict suggests, we must always maintain the balance between the natural priority of birth and the natural giftedness in our children. Seeing each one for his own intrinsic worth will grant the best to all.

CHAPTER LXII
THE PRIESTS OF THE MONASTERY

If an Abbot wishes to have a priest or deacon ordained for his service, he should choose from his monks one who is fit to exercise the priesthood. He who is ordained, however, must beware of elation or pride and he should not take upon himself any work that has not been committed to him by the Abbot.

He should realise that he is all the more bound to submit to monastic discipline. Nor on account of his priesthood should he forget the obedience and the discipline of the Rule, but he should go forward more and more towards God.

Let him always keep the position corresponding to his entry into the monastery, except when officiating at the altar, unless the choice of the community and the will of the Abbot promote him to a higher station on account of the merit of his life. He should realise that he is bound by the rule laid down for deans and priors; if he presumes to behave otherwise, the judgement will be passed not on the priest but on the rebellion. If after frequent warnings he does not mend his ways, the Bishop also should be called in as a witness against him. If, even so, he does not amend and his faults are manifest, he must be expelled from the monastery – that is if his stubbornness is such that he will neither submit nor obey the Rule.

❧

Here Benedict continues to deal with the pecking order within the community. In modern monasteries most of the monks are also ordained priests. In Benedict's day they remained laymen. If one is chosen to exercise a priestly ministry, Benedict is clear that this does not make him any better than the other brothers. Indeed, by virtue of his sacred calling, the priest 'should realise that he is all the more bound to submit to monastic discipline'.

In chapter two Benedict has made it clear that the abbot's authority resides in the fact that he too is under obedience to the rule of Christ, and that he can expect his monks to do nothing which he as abbot does not himself already live by. The same applies to the priest in the community. Jesus told the disciples that they should be even better than the law-abiding Pharisees (Matt. 5.20). Just as the disciples were to go beyond the letter of the law and live in the spirit of the law, so the priest in Benedict's community must use the Rule to 'go forward more and more towards God'.

This is true of anyone in a position of leadership, whether in business, in the home or in the Church. Leaders must be masters of theory. They must know the ropes. They must live by their own precepts or their leadership is worthless. So in the home, our children will always be watching. If they catch us even in one seemingly harmless lie we will be tainted for ever in their minds, and if we do not deal with the inconsistency our authority will begin to disintegrate and all their ideals may crumble. The responsibility therefore is awesome, and we cannot fulfil the calling of Christian fatherhood without divine assistance.

So to help us bear the burden of this responsibility Benedict advises the leader to take seriously his commitment to obedience, and his reliance on the order within the community. It is within the structure of obedience that we can lead others successfully. It is within the order of community that our own lives are best ordered. Finally, within the larger context respect for the order within the community is the best way for us to establish and maintain that stability which is at the heart of the Benedictine way.

CHAPTER LXIII
THE ORDER OF THE COMMUNITY (A)

The time of their entering monastic life, their personal merits, and the decision of the Abbot, shall decide the order which they keep in the monastery. Yet the Abbot must not upset the flock entrusted to him, nor should he make any unjust arrangement as though he were free to give orders as he pleases, for he must always bear in mind that he is going to have to render an account of all his decisions and actions. In the order, then, which he has laid down, or which they otherwise have among themselves, shall the brethren come to the kiss of peace, or to Communion, or intone a Psalm or occupy their place in choir. In no circumstances or places is age to decide order or have any bearing upon it, for the youthful Samuel and Daniel acted as judges over their elders. Therefore, with the exception of those whom, as we have said, the Abbot has promoted or degraded for definite reasons, the rest are to take their places according to the time of their coming to the monastery; for example, one who has entered the monastery at the second hour is to know that he is junior to him who entered at the first, whatever his age or dignity. For the boys, however, all have the task of keeping order wherever they are.

Benedict recognizes the need for order within his Christian community. But this order has nothing to do with the social hierarchy outside the monastery. All precedence of age, nobility, accomplishment, race or education is left at the door. Here the only rule of placement is the date of entrance to the monastery. So a young monk may be 'further up' than an old man who has just joined.

But Benedict doesn't establish a rule of order simply to help communal life run efficiently. He wants the monks to 'know their place' both outwardly and inwardly. In a world where the ambitious rule and we are tempted to climb the greasy pole of success it is not easy to 'know our place'. And yet knowing our place is another way of knowing ourselves. Seeking worldly advancement cuts us off from our roots and from our real selves, and such a condition is disastrous for the soul. Benedict realizes that self-knowledge is vital if we are to make spiritual progress. He also knows that we can only come to know ourselves through stability and humility. Establishing an order in the monastery based on the date of each monk's total commitment to Christ nurtures stability because the order doesn't change. Humility is nurtured because former precedence has gone and they have all begun at the bottom. So the order of precedence which is lived out through such mundane things as procession into choir is Benedict's way to engrain stability and humility in each monk.

If we are attempting to learn our 'place' in life, then it follows that we must help our children learn their place too. Sometimes this means putting them down, but more often it means raising them up. So in the parable of the wedding feast the master tells one guest to move down, but lovingly invites another to 'come up higher' (Luke 14.7–11). Likewise in the simple day-to-day routine of family life children need to be corrected and trained to know their rightful place. If we don't do this our children will be inclined to think too highly of themselves on the one hand, and not well enough of themselves on the other. They need an objective outside observer to help them discover their true identity and 'place' in life. This lifelong task begins in the family. Benedict mentions this too when he says the boys have always to keep their proper order.

CHAPTER LXIII
THE ORDER OF THE COMMUNITY (B)

*Juniors, therefore, must show respect for their seniors, and seniors must love their juniors. In calling one another by name it is not allowed to anyone to use the name alone; seniors should address their juniors by the name of brother; juniors should address their seniors as **Nonnus**, by which is signified the reverence due to a father. The Abbot, however, as he is believed to act in the place of Christ, should be called Lord and Abbot, not because he demands these titles, but for the honour and love of Christ. He himself must bear this in mind, and show himself worthy of such honour.*

Whenever the brethren meet one another, the junior should seek a blessing of the elder. A younger monk should rise and offer the seat to an older one if he passes by, nor should he venture to sit down again, unless the older one tells him to, so that it may be as it is written, 'Forestall one another in paying honour.'

Children and youths are to keep their places, in good order, in the oratory and at table. Out of doors also and anywhere at all they should be under supervision and discipline, until they reach an age that can understand.

❦

When monks process into choir they come in order of precedence, bowing to one another in respect as they enter the sanctuary. So they hint at the almost Oriental ritualistic courtesy which Benedict expounds in today's reading.

Having established the necessary criteria for order in the monastery, he now explains how the order of precedence is to be expressed. Children and young people are always to keep their places in respect. Older monks are to bless the younger, the younger to stand and offer respect to the older. All are to revere the abbot as Christ.

Benedict doesn't establish these rules of courtesy and respect simply to lubricate the difficulties of living together. Instead, they are practical ways for the monks to express their rightful place in the community. So through courtesy they accept stability and express love in a formal way. Since our love for one another should be a reflection of God's unconditional and objective love for us, there is room for our love to be expressed through objective routines of courtesy and respect. Thomas Aquinas defines love as 'wishing the best for another person'. Outward courtesies are ways of expressing those good wishes in a way which is routine, and yet meaningful.

In this chapter Benedict mentions how we express this Christian love in a formal way through the kiss of peace at Mass. This is meant to be a liturgical gesture – a formal sign of the objective love of God which flows through us to others. When it becomes a chatty time of bonhomie and forced cheerfulness the whole exercise becomes shallow and misses the point.

If a measure of Benedictine courtesy belongs in the Mass it also belongs in our own business life, schools and families. In this sloppy age we can all do with an increase in common courtesy and genuine good manners. Within the family we should train the children not to scream at one another and especially not at us as parents. They should express themselves, but do so with restraint and respect. Children should also learn to speak and behave respectfully in the presence of older people. From a practical point of view, good manners are worth pursuing because obnoxious children soon become boorish adults. Benedict says this too: 'Children are to keep their places in good order at the table and the oratory'.

CHAPTER LXIV
THE INSTITUTION OF THE ABBOT (A)

This principle must always be kept in mind in the institution of the Abbot: he should be appointed whom the united community chooses in the fear of God, or whom a smaller part of the community chooses with the sounder judgement. He who is to be appointed must be chosen on account of his virtuous life and wise teaching, even if he is the last in order in the community. So that even if (may it not happen!) the whole community should with one accord elect a person who will connive at their defects, and if these defects somehow become known to the Bishop to whose diocese the place belongs, and to the local abbots or christians, they should put a stop to this plot of wicked men, and set a worthy steward over the household of God. And they should know that they will receive a good reward if they act with a pure intention and zeal for God, and that on the other hand it would be sinful to neglect their duty.

❧

The monks are given a say in choosing their abbot, but within the Christian family the only member of the community we can choose is our spouse. It is good to remember that when our wives chose us they were not choosing a fully-formed, tried and tested husband and father for their children. They chose us more for our potential than because we were fully mature and responsible men. Benedict also advises his monks to look for potential. The nominee for abbot should exhibit wise teaching and good life. They must choose a man who can become a 'worthy steward'.

The job of being a Christian father is summed up in the picture of the good steward, and the Scriptures are full of 'good steward' imagery. In the Old Testament Joseph was a good steward in Pharaoh's household. He was loyal, diligent and exercised careful foresight. St Joseph, the husband of the Blessed Virgin, offers another excellent role model. The New Testament tells us he was 'a good man' and his actions show his careful planning and provision for Mary and Jesus.

In his parables Jesus commends the steward who is shrewd (Luke 16.1–8), the steward who is faithful (Luke 12.42–47), and the one who uses wisely all the gifts that are given to him (Matt. 25.14–30). There are two attitudes of the steward which we should remember. First, the good steward is always conscious that he is set over a household which is not his own. It is one of Benedict's constant themes that all our belongings and family have been lent, not given. We are not to lord it over others, or cling to material things, for they really don't belong to us. We are merely the stewards of the household, servants looking after the Master's goods. This leads to the second point: the good steward is constantly aware that he answers to a master. The steward who looks for his master's return is one who is awake and alert (Luke 12.36–37). In the first lines of the Rule Benedict has called us to wake up and stay alert; so the good steward is always conscious of the presence of the Lord. Because of that constant presence he can never become slack, arrogant or dictatorial in the home. It is only this daily, prayerful alertness to the presence of Christ which makes us faithful stewards of the household God has given (1 Pet. 4.10).

CHAPTER LXIV

THE INSTITUTION OF THE ABBOT (B)

When he has been instituted, the Abbot should always bear in mind what a burden he has undertaken, and to whom he will have to render an account of his stewardship. He should know, too, that he ought to be of profit to his brethren rather than just preside over them. He ought, therefore, to be learned in the divine law, so that he may know it well, and that if may be for him a store whence he draws forth new things and old. He should be a chaste man, temperate and merciful. He should always prefer mercy to judgement, that he may also obtain mercy. Let him hate sin, let him love the brethren.

⟳

Benedict here gives us further insights into the character of the good and loving *abba*. Key to the whole chapter is the little line, 'he ought to be of profit to his brethren, rather than just preside over them'. So his attempts to be chaste, temperate and merciful are not for his own good, but for the welfare and 'profit' of his family.

Once again Benedict's tenderness is shown as he reminds us how to discipline our children. We must always prefer mercy to punishment. While we must hate the sin we must always love the sinner. Our children are like delicate vessels: we mustn't rub too hard to get rid of the rust lest we break the pot. We must be aware that our own frailty and loss of temper will often infect our judgement. We must not be fussy, stubborn or suspicious. Most of all we must always aim to be loved rather than feared.

But if this is the portrait of the loving *abba* then it is also a precise and tender picture of God's dealings with us. As we meditate on this chapter we are brought to a profound understanding of God's patient care for us. As we look back through our own lives we will see just how delicately God has treated us. Despite our disobedience, our stubborn wilfulness and disastrous mistakes he has been there to guide, watch and correct us with all gentleness and concern. He has given us every opportunity to carry more while never giving so much that we become discouraged and quit running the race.

Finally, if we see God the Father in Benedict's portrait of the loving *abba*, then it becomes clear how vital it is for us to emulate Benedict's *abba* within our families. Some people don't like talking of God as Father because they believe too many people have had bad fathers and cannot relate well to God as Father. But it can work the other way: God the Father can fill in and make up for bad human fathers. Furthermore, if there has been an epidemic of bad fathering, all the more reason for us to reverse that trend. It is a humbling truth that our children will think of God as us writ large. It is imperative therefore that we give them an accurate glimpse of God through our father–child relationship within the family. This is only possible if we first know what God is like ourselves, and to do this we must cultivate a good relationship with him. Everything else flows from that source of everlasting love.

CHAPTER LXV
THE PRIOR OF THE MONASTERY (A)

It happens fairly often that serious scandals occur in monasteries because of the appointment of a Prior; for there are those who, swelling up with an evil spirit of pride, consider themselves second abbots, act like tyrants and nourish scandals and quarrels in the community. This happens especially in places where the Prior is appointed by the same Bishop or by the same abbots as appoint the Abbot of the monastery. It is easy to see how unwise this is: for from the very beginning of his appointment the Prior is given grounds for waxing proud, since his thoughts suggest to him that he is exempt from the Abbot's authority, because, 'You have been appointed by the same persons as the Abbot.' Hence arise envy, quarrels, detraction, rivalries, dissensions and disorders; for while the Abbot and Prior are in opposition to each other, of necessity their own souls are endangered by this quarrelling, and also those under their authority, seeking favour from one side or the other, head for perdition. The evils arising from such a dangerous state of affairs are due primarily to those who have been the originators of such a disorder.

It is easy to read Benedict's Rule and imagine that life in the monastery is like heaven on earth. Perhaps this commentary has also sometimes painted a picture of Christian family life which is perfectly easy and peaceful. But both the Rule and the commentary point us to an ideal. This chapter reminds us that neither monastic life nor family life is quite so easy. Any community is made up of very imperfect sinners. The selfishness which breeds chaos, rebellion and strife is always brewing just below the surface.

For Benedict the source of trouble is often the prior. It is not easy to play second fiddle. The prior may well be a capable man whose ambitions have been frustrated. As such he will become the focus and source of other discontent in the community, and before long factions have arisen and civil war breaks out. This scenario is well known to anyone who has made a serious effort to build community within a parish, a home or an extended family.

Within our own families the disruption is most likely to break out between the husband and wife. When the parents quarrel, the children are automatically involved. As Benedict points out, the whole community soon disintegrates into rivalry, envy, factions and infighting. Often one parent will side with the children and even seek to turn them against the other parent. Even when that doesn't consciously happen the children will invariably side with one parent or other, so that quarrelling always leads to division and civil war.

Just as Benedict places the abbot in the place of responsibility, so it is our role as *abba* in the family to make sure there is harmony and reconciliation after a dispute. Most men wish for a quiet life and will sit back and let their wives take charge. This is irresponsible. We must be proactive, sensing a dispute that is brewing and taking steps to prevent it. If there is a quarrel, then it is our job to get involved to sort it out objectively and fairly. When a quarrel is over the *abba* should take the steps towards reconciliation and renewal. Sometimes this will mean our own humiliation. We may have to lead the way and apologize to our wife or children first. Conflict in the home is a fact of life and we must fight the instinct to run away from it. Conflict is a challenge to be overcome: no one wins by running away.

CHAPTER LXV
THE PRIOR OF THE MONASTERY (B)

For this reason we think it expedient for the preservation of peace and charity that the making of appointments in the monastery should depend on the Abbot's judgement and, if it is possible, that all the business of the monastery should be carried on through deans, under the control of the Abbot, as we have already laid down. Thus no one may wax proud over what is committed to many.

If, however, local conditions require it, or the community makes a reasonable and humble request, and the Abbot judges it to be expedient, then the Abbot himself should appoint as his Prior whomsoever he chooses after taking the advice of God-fearing brethren. For his part the Prior is to perform respectfully whatever functions the Abbot lays upon him, and do nothing contrary to his will or arrangements. For inasmuch as he has been placed over others, he should the more carefully keep the precepts of the Rule. If it should turn out that the Prior has serious faults or, deceived by vanity, acts arrogantly, or it turns out that he is a belittler of the Holy Rule, he should be verbally rebuked up to four times; if he does not then change his ways, he should be punished according to the disciplinary code. If, however, he does not amend even so, then he must be deposed from his office as Prior, and another who is suitable for it be put in his place. And if afterwards he does not live quietly and obediently among the community, he should even be expelled from the monastery.

The Abbot should, however, bear in mind the account he must render to God for all his decisions, for fear that the flame of jealousy or evil zeal burn in his soul.

In the second half of his chapter on troublesome priors, Benedict explores the ways of resolving the disputes. Ideally the abbot will chose a colleague he can work with as his prior. But if the prior still turns out to be rebellious then he must be warned four times, then deposed from office, and if he still can't live in peace in the community he is to be expelled from the monastery.

This part of the Rule is a good reminder that, while Benedict is always tender and gentle in his approach to discipline, he also believes in firmness. He will not stop until a problem is solved and will take whatever means necessary to get rid of trouble in the community. At the same time he reminds the abbot to examine himself and always be on guard against his own jealousy and desire for power.

Within the home a similar resolve is needed. As Christian husbands and fathers it is all too easy to let small faults slip by when the children are young. Their wrongdoing seems fairly harmless so we turn a blind eye. Taking corrective measures seems too strict. But the patterns of good behaviour need to be established early. If we neglect their bad behaviour when they are young we pay dearly for it later. Better to be strict then soft rather than soft then strict.

Benedict is both firm and persistent. He watches the troublesome prior to see if the discipline is working. If not, another step is taken against his rebellion. So a particular problem in our marriage or family may need our attention over a long period of time. We mustn't yield just because a particular bramble bush is especially thorny and deep-rooted. The weed has to be rooted out – the deeply-rooted ones especially because they will be the ones which bear the bitterest fruit.

But if we are intent on weeding the garden of our

marriage and family, we must expect our wives and children to be doing a similar work in our own lives. We must listen to them and accept criticism. Benedict reminds the abbot always to attend to the state of his own heart lest the weeds he is rooting out of others have taken root in his own life. We must do the same.

CHAPTER LXVI
THE DOORKEEPERS OF THE MONASTERY

At the gate of the monastery, a wise old man is to be posted, one capable of receiving a message and giving a reply, and whose maturity guarantees that he will not wander round. This doorkeeper should have a cell near the gate, so that persons who arrive may always find someone at hand to give them a reply. As soon as anyone knocks, or a poor man calls out, he should answer 'Thanks be to God' or 'God bless you'. Then with all the gentleness that comes from the fear of God, he should speedily and with the warmth of charity attend to the enquirer.

If the doorkeeper needs it, he should have a younger brother to help him.

If it is possible, the monastery should be organised so that all its needs, that is to say things such as water, a mill, a garden, and various crafts, may be met within its premises, so that the monks have no need to wander round outside it, for that does not profit their souls at all. This Rule we wish to be read frequently in the community, so that none of the brethren may plead ignorance of it.

❧

This chapter is reminiscent of one of those scenes of light relief in Shakespeare. Benedict's old doorkeeper is a lovable, almost comical figure like the porter in Macbeth. As such, the old monk's gentle goodness is a delightful contrast to the bitterness of the ambitious prior in the chapter before. The porter has a cell near the outside world, but there is no fear of his wandering away. He is constantly alert for the knock on the door; remembering that the guest is to be welcomed as Christ, he calls out a blessing and goes as quickly as possible to welcome him in.

This chapter may have been the original ending of the Rule because it finishes with a short command to read the Rule frequently in the monastery. If so, then the placement of the doorkeeper at the end is significant because the old porter becomes a parting portrait of the ideal monk. The old man is a picture of what all the monks should aim for. He is firmly rooted in the monastery, but always looks outward in concern for the outside world. He may have had important jobs in his youth, but now he is humble enough to take the lowly job of porter. But in his wisdom he imbues that job with a profound significance, for like the faithful steward he is always alert to the coming of Christ. He welcomes others as a blessing, not a nuisance, so his greeting of 'Thanks be to God' or 'God bless you!' is a sign of the inner transformation which has taken place in his life. In his simplicity the old doorkeeper is the ideal Benedictine; he is an embodiment of stability, obedience and conversion of life.

We might be inclined to think that such peace and gentle goodness is easy for an old man who doesn't have the daily stress of family life. But old age has its own pains and troubles and there are plenty of grumpy and sour old men who show that romantic notion to be an illusion. In fact, to acquire and maintain the profound peace and gentle goodness of the old doorkeeper is tough at any age. The old doorman is only perfect because of his lifetime of running the race. So we are constructing the kind of old man we will be here and now. We might become peaceful, gentle and wise in old age if we seek gentleness, peace and wisdom now: otherwise there's not a chance.

CHAPTER LXVII
BRETHREN SENT ON A JOURNEY

Brethren who are being sent on a journey are to commend them-selves to the prayers of all the brethren and of the Abbot; and in the final prayer of the Work of God there should be a commemo-ration of all who are absent. When brethren return from a journey, at all the canonical hours of the day on which they return, they should lie prostrate on the floor of the oratory, as the Work of God comes to an end, and ask for the prayers of all, for any faults that may have overtaken them on their journey, such as the sight or hearing of an evil thing or idle chatter. No one should venture to tell another anything he may have seen or heard while outside the monastery, for that does much harm. But if anyone does this he must undergo punishment according to the Rule. The same thing applies to anyone who dares to go out of the enclosure of the monastery, or to go anywhere, or do anything, although of small importance, without the approval of the Abbot.

☙

When brothers leave the monastery they are sent off with prayer and received with prayer. In Benedict's day the outside world was a lawless world of danger. But Benedict sees the spiritual peril outside the monastery as well. When the brothers return they are to confess the sinful things they have seen or done while away. Furthermore, they are not to speak of what they have seen outside the enclosure.

We may not wish to develop quite the 'fortress mentality' that Benedict does, but it does no harm to think of our home as a refuge from the sinful outside world. It has never been more vital for our children to be protected from all sorts of threats, both physical and spiritual. But at the same time we have to be careful not to protect them too much. They must be shielded from the world, but they must also learn to deal with the real world successfully. The father's role in this process is all-important, for it is traditionally the father more than the mother who is the bridge to the outside world. He is the one who copes with the outside world and teaches the children to do the same. This task should be taken on with practicality and initiative. We should help children learn how to handle money, how to work hard and look for opportunities. We should also take time to teach them how to communicate well with those outside the home and relate with both their superiors and those beneath them.

This chapter also shows us the proper spiritual attitude to the outside world. Like the brothers going on a journey, we are all pilgrims and transients in this world. As Christians our home is a city not made with a hands, eternal in the heavens (Heb. 11.8–10; 13.14). We must live and work and minister in the world, but we mustn't put our tent pegs too deep, because we are citizens of another country (Eph. 2.19). Each day that the family goes out into the world on the day's journey we should begin with prayers for blessing and protection. On our return at night we should examine our conscience and give prayers of thanks. This binds us together, keeps us unsoiled by the world and keeps our eyes fixed on our eternal home whose maker and builder is God.

CHAPTER LXVIII
IF A BROTHER IS SET IMPOSSIBLE TASKS

If it should happen that burdensome or impossible tasks are imposed on one of the brethren he should indeed accept with complete calm and obedience the command of the one who so orders, but if he sees that the weight of the burden quite exceeds the limits of his strength, he should quietly and at a suitable moment explain to his superior the reasons why he cannot do it, not in a proud way nor with the spirit of resistance, or contradiction. But if after his explanations the one in authority remains firm in requiring what he has ordered, the junior must understand that this is what is best for him, and let him lovingly trust in God's aid, and so obey.

In his chapter on obedience Benedict has made it clear that the monk must obey instantly and without question. But Benedict is never happy with hard answers. Throughout the Rule he constantly reminds us that the abbot must be aware of human weakness and never give anything too burdensome. So in this chapter he sets out guidelines for dialogue. If a monk feels some command really is impossible, then he may say so in a genuine spirit of humility and submission.

The principle here is that rules are one thing and reality another. In our own life we may find some rules of the Church seem impossible to keep. Mindless obedience accomplishes little, but if we question the rule it must not be done in a spirit of pride and rebellion. Instead our first instinct must be to understand the rule and try our hardest to obey it. But if the rule is truly impossible then we should consult our spiritual father for advice. In a spirit of humility and submission we should state our case. He may be able to show us a way to ease the burden while still obeying, or he may see that the particular rule in our situation is actually hindering some greater obedience to which we are called. At the heart of the matter is our attitude. Do we object out of stubbornness and pride or because we really cannot bear the burden?

Within the family Benedict's Rule is also useful. We must not expect mindless obedience from our children. We should explain what we want and why we want it. Obedience is much easier when we understand the reason for the command. Sometimes instant obedience is necessary, but likewise, we should allow children the opportunity to discuss a request they find difficult. This openess makes for a more peaceful and fair family life. But it also prevents them nursing a grudge. Furthermore, if they learn how to discuss their problems properly they will learn valuable communication and problem-solving skills for later life. Rather than mindless, grudging obedience they will have learned how to interact properly with their superiors, and that skill and confidence will enable them to take positions of leadership when it is appropriate.

April 27
August 27
December 27

CHAPTER LXIX
THAT IN THE MONASTERY ONE MUST NOT DEFEND ANOTHER

Let it be noted that in the monastery no monk may assume the right to defend or act as a kind of protector to another for any reason whatever, even if they are connected by a bond blood-relationship. Monks must not presume to do this in any way, for from it may arise the possibility of very grave scandals. If anyone offends in this respect he must be sharply dealt with.

In any community it is easy to take sides with a person who seems to have been wronged. Benedict is quick to root this out. Not even natural kinsmen may take sides. He knows that this kind of favouritism leads to backbiting and self-pity. Furthermore, misery loves company, so the disgruntled pair will soon seek other grumblers and before long a faction will be formed and the community will be divided.

Taking sides is wrong for several reasons. Firstly, it is a kind of false judgement. We rarely know the whole story in any conflict, and we too often read our own particular agenda into someone else's situation. In addition, taking sides is usually evidence of a deeper rebellion within the one who supports the 'underdog'. The supporter probably has a chip on his shoulder against the authority figure. Thirdly, taking sides often does the other wrongdoer no favours either. It encourages their self-pity and prevents the proper process of contrition and reconciliation. Finally, a friendship formed in such circumstances is fuelled on grumbling and negativity. It will therefore always be a destructive alliance.

But while Benedict doesn't allow monks to take sides with an offender he does make provision in chapter twenty-seven for wise and gentle brothers to go to the person and 'take their side' in a proper way. The abbot sends a comforter to the offending monk to comfort him, listen to his side of the story and encourage his contrition and reconciliation.

Within the family this same procedure should be followed. If one child is disciplined we mustn't allow him to nurse his grudge by having a grumbling session with his brother or sister. That only nurtures discontent and dissent. But neither must we let the disciplined child suffer in complete solitude. Most often the other parent should be the one who consoles and helps the child to get over the upset. At the same time parents must never appear to contradict one another and take the side of the child against the other parent. It is possible to console and reconcile the child while still supporting the disciplinary action which has been taken. In every circumstance Benedict encourages a firm but gentle discipline which not only helps the individual, but also contributes to the peace and welfare of the whole community. So in our families the discipline must be fair but firm, and it must build up everyone and tear down no one.

CHAPTER LXX
THAT NO ONE MAY HIT ANOTHER

All outbreaks of self-assertiveness are to be avoided in the monastery. We therefore lay down that no one is allowed to excommunicate or strike any of his brethren, unless the Abbot has given him authority to do so. 'Those who offend must be rebuked in the presence of all, so that the rest may be warned.' Care, however, and supervision are to be shown by everyone with regard to the discipline of children up to fifteen years of age, yet with all moderation and good sense. With regard to those who are older than that, if anyone presumes to take action without the Abbot's instruction, or gets angry and behaves without discretion to the children also, he must submit to the discipline of the Rule, for it is written, 'Do not to another what you would not have done to yourself.

⬥

Chapters sixty-seven to seventy-two form a kind of appendix to the original Rule. As such they provide some detail and qualification to what Benedict has already laid down. So while Benedict has elsewhere commended corporal punishment – especially for the boys – he now reminds the monks that all discipline is to be carried out by the proper authority and that it must never be done in anger or self-assertiveness. The community is to enact the discipline together under the abbot's supervision.

Especially telling for us is his instruction, 'Care,

however, and supervision are to be shown by everyone with regard to the discipline of children up to fifteen years of age, yet with all moderation and good sense'. If anyone gets angry and behaves without discretion towards the children they are to be disciplined themselves. Benedict is aware that children are also individuals in their own right. They should be honoured and respected and never abused. Part of Benedict's wisdom is to see that force accomplishes nothing positive. Each person must make their own choice to obey and grow spiritually. Discipline can only encourage and channel that personal choice.

Benedict gives the impression in this chapter that the whole community must work together to avoid lashing out in anger towards one another and to the children. So in the family we must work together to avoid the anger that so quickly destroys our relationships. If one of us hits a child in anger the other spouse should correct them for it later. We often think verbal abuse is better than a smack. It can be argued that it is actually worse because the damage is deeper and more permanent. Within the family it is often tempting to turn away from the anger of another person, to leave the room and escape the rage. But such escapism won't do. If one member of the family is in a temper we must wade in and try to defuse the explosive situation. The angry person must leave the room to cool off and we must take charge. Together the whole family must find a way to solve the problem before it gets worse. Then when the time is right we must give a sharp rebuke to the angry person so they can see what emotional damage their rage is inflicting on the rest of the family. If we're giving way to bad temper then we must instruct our wives to tell us off if we need it.

CHAPTER LXXI
THAT THE BRETHREN OBEY
ONE ANOTHER

The goodness of obedience is not to be shown only through obedi-
ence to the Abbot, but the brethren should also obey each other,
in the knowledge that by this path of obedience they will draw
nearer God. The commands of the Abbot or of the superiors
appointed by him must come first and we do not allow personal
demands to be attended to before them, but otherwise all the
younger monks should obey the older ones with all love and care.
And if anyone is found to be contentious, he should be corrected.
And if, for any reason at all, a brother is corrected in any way by
the Abbot or by an elder, or if he perceives that the feelings of any
elder have been roused to anger against him, even slightly, he
should at once and without delay prostrate himself at his feet
and lie there in sign of reparation until the rift is healed by a
blessing. If anyone is too proud to do this, he must either
undergo corporal punishment or, if he is contumacious, he must
be put out of the monastery.

❧

Benedict complements his earlier teaching on obedience
by exhorting the monks not only to obey the abbot, but
also to obey one another in love. This chapter gives a ratio-
nale for the whole monastic life, indeed for any Christian
community from the nuclear family up to the whole of
society. In Benedict's terms the ideal is one of mutual
obedience. It can also be seen as mutual service. In other

words all of us, according to our place, need to serve and obey others. If we have caused any offence then we should humbly seek instant reconciliation.

The command of obedience is first to Christ our Lord. The monk obeys the abbot as Christ and the ideal of mutual obedience in the Christian community flows from that primary obedience. Benedict follows the gospel in teaching that we revere Christ in others, so to serve Christ is to serve others. So also to obey others is to obey Christ, and the two primary commands to love God and love our neighbour are fulfilled.

Such service puts flesh on the promise to pursue obedience, stability and conversion of life, for as we serve others the fulfilment of those three vows is unavoidable. To obey others fully we must also ask what that obedience consists of. This 'obedience' is based in love, and love is the profound desire for the good of another person. So our service to others consists of doing and saying whatever is best for them. This is not easy since whatever is best for them may not be what they actually want, or what we find easy to deliver. Nevertheless, this is the radical kind of mutual obedience which Benedict offers as the Christian ideal.

The ideal is difficult in any setting. Living out such a love is no easier in the monastery than it is anywhere. As laymen we aim to live out this ideal within our workplace, our parish, and especially our home. The root of the word 'obey' is 'to listen' so the first point of obeying others is to listen intently to their needs. But every moment of the day our own selfish desires intrude and war against the idea that we should think of others and seek to obey them. Two things balance this impossible ideal. Firstly, we can only obey others in an environment where others are also trying to support the ideal. Secondly, we cannot even begin to live out such an ideal in our own strength, so the primary monastic prayer, 'O God come to my assistance; O Lord make haste to help me', must always be on our lips and in our heart.

CHAPTER LXXII
ON THE GOOD ZEAL WHICH MONKS OUGHT TO HAVE

As there is an evil zeal rooted in bitterness which separates from God and leads to hell, so there is a good zeal which separates from vice and leads to God and to eternal life. This, therefore, is the zeal which monks should practise with the most ardent love, in other words, they should forestall one another in paying honour. They should with the greatest patience make allowance for one another's weaknesses, whether physical or moral. They should rival one another in practising obedience. No one should pursue what he thinks advantageous for himself, but rather what seems best for another. They should labour with chaste love at the charity of the brotherhood. They should fear God. They should love their Abbot with sincere and humble charity. They should prefer nothing whatever to Christ.

May he bring us all alike to life everlasting.

❧

In this final chapter Benedict points us to the very heart of the matter. The Rule is only a guide-book. The monk's life is to be fired with a zeal for goodness which separates him from sin and leads to God and eternal life. This zeal manifests itself in an ardent love, a love which pays honour to others, forgives weaknesses and constantly initiates a dynamic and joyful obedience to the abbot and the whole community. The whole spirit of the Rule is summed up in Benedict's parting phrases: 'They should prefer nothing whatever to Christ'.

This zeal or 'ardent love' is a gift. One may try as hard as possible to have this love and zeal but it will be shallow and false. Nothing is worse than the religious person who is trying hard to reproduce real spiritual passion, zeal and love. These are the ones who talk big, plaster on their 'holy grins' and cultivate a shallow religious bonhomie complete with hugs and pretended concern. The reason Benedict keeps the chapter on zeal for the end is because true zeal and ardent love are too rare and precious to deal with early in the Rule. So first he sets up the rules to live by, then says that the secret is this gift of love, this genius which enlivens every rule, fulfils every command and forgives every defect in one divine action of grace.

But if he keeps the secret of zeal to the end it is also because the zeal and the Rule are linked together. True zeal and ardent love are truly a gift, but the gift is most likely to be received by the person who has been following Benedict's Rule and following the way of obedience, stability and conversion of life. So the Rule prepares the soul to receive the gift of zeal and ardent love.

This is the whole aim of our lives here on earth: to prepare ourselves to receive the gift of divine love, for this love is the gift of Christ himself who promises to dwell in our hearts and be one with us. If we follow the path Benedict sets before us, then the gift will in time be given. Then it will be completely natural for us to 'prefer nothing whatever to Christ'. Then we will experience Benedict's offer of joy for we will 'run in the path of God's commandments, our hearts overflowing with an inexpressible delight of love'.

CHAPTER LXXIII
THE WHOLE KEEPING OF JUSTICE IS NOT COVERED BY THIS RULE

*We have written this Rule so that by following it in monasteries, we may to some extent show that we lead blameless lives and possess a beginning of the monastic way of life. In addition there are for him who would hasten to the perfection of the monastic ways the doctrines of the holy Fathers, which, if a man keeps them, will lead to the height of perfection. For is not every page of the Old or New Testament, every word of the Divine Author, a most direct rule for our human life? Does not every book of the Catholic Fathers proclaim that we should make our way by the most direct path to our Creator? There are also the **Conferences**, and **Institutes**, and the **Lives of the Fathers**, and the **Rule** of the holy Father Basil. What are these works but aids to the attainment of virtue for good-living and obedient monks? But to us who are slothful, who live badly and who are negligent, they bring a blush of shame. Whoever you are, then, who are hurrying forward to your heavenly fatherland, do you with Christ's help fulfil this little Rule written for beginners; and then you will come at the end, under God's protection, to those heights of learning and virtue which we have mentioned above. Amen.*

❦

Benedict concludes with a postscript and a list for further reading. In a truly humble phrase he suggests that his Rule is only a 'little Rule written for beginners', and he goes on to recommend deeper reading from the Scriptures, and from the writings of the apostolic fathers, as well as other monastic writers. Nevertheless he does offer his 'little Rule' as a help for anyone who is hurrying to heaven. If they fulfil the Rule, with Christ's help they may come at last to those heights of virture and learning which Benedict has held before them. Benedict calls his Rule a 'little Rule' in true modesty, but it is also a 'little Rule' because at its very heart it offers a way to sanctity which is very similar to another 'little way' offered by a very different saint at a very different time. It is Thérèse of Lisieux who also offered us a 'little way' – a way of humility that all can follow.

The way of both saints is 'little' because it puts humility and obedience at the heart of the soul's pursuit. This way is 'little' because it is deeply rooted in the most mundane and ordinary things of life. We have seen how Benedict roots the spiritual in our treatment of tools, our approach to food and drink, our execution of duty, our attitude to work and especially our treatment of others. This way is 'little' because it seeks heaven in ordinary and proclaims that holiness is to be found where we are. As the poet Henry Vaughan has written:

> here in dust and dirt, O here
> The lilies of his love appear.

But this is also a 'little' way because it can be followed by anyone. The Benedictine monk or nun follows the letter of the Rule, but anyone may pursue the spirit of the Rule according to their place in life, for all of us have to deal with the challenge of community, material things, work, and prayer. Finally, this way is a 'little' way because it can also be understood and followed by the 'little' people in our life – our children.

As Christian fathers it is our duty and joy to encourage our children to 'run the path of God's commandments'. The way of St Benedict is an ideal help in that task, for

Benedict's blend of practical wisdom and spiritual insight equips us for the task of helping our wives and children to see and respond to 'God's mighty hand in all his works'. By immersing ourselves in this Rule we will find a joyful way to obey God, we will establish a new stability in our lives and we will ultimately go through that inner conversion of life which is no less than an utter transformation into the radiant image of Christ himself.

FURTHER READING

Esther de Waal, *Seeking God – The Way of St Benedict*, Fount Paperbacks, 1984.

Esther de Waal, *A Life-Giving Way: A Commentary on the Rule of St Benedict*, Collegeville, Liturgical Press, 1995.

Daniel Rees, *Consider Your Call – A Theology of the Monastic Life Today*, SPCK, 1978.

Columba Stewart OSB, *Prayer and Community – The Benedictine Tradition*, Darton, Longman & Todd, 1998.

Columba Cary-Elwes and Catherine Wybourne, *Work and Prayer – The Rule of St Benedict for Lay People*, Burns & Oates, 1992.

Catherine de Hueck Doherty, *Poustinia*, Fount Paperbacks, 1975.

Thomas Merton, *The Wisdom of the Desert*, Sheldon Press, 1960.

David Knowles, *The Benedictines*, Sheed & Ward, 1929.

Dolores Leckey, *The Ordinary Way – A Family Spirituality*, Crossroad, 1982.

David Hugh Farmer, *Benedict's Disciples*, Gracewing, 1995.

CPSIA information can be obtained
at www.ICGtesting.com
Printed in the USA
LVHW042106180920
666522LV00001B/4